bright lights

dark nights

**The enduring faith of 13
remarkable Australians**

bright
lights
dark
nights

blue bottle
BOOKS

Blue Bottle Books
P.O Box A287
Sydney South NSW 1235

Ph: (612) 8268 3344
Fax: (612) 8268 3357

E: sales@youthworks.net
W: www.publications.youthworks.net

Published August 2008
Copyright © Blue Bottle Books

National Library of Australia
ISBN 978-1-921460-10-4

Cover and typesetting by
Richard Knight Design

For Michele

Acknowledgments

I would like to thank the people at Blue Bottle Books, especially Rhonda Watson, for having the foresight and imagination to adopt the concept, Desiree O'Farrell, for her encouragement to take it on, and Julie Firmstone, for the practicalities involved in bringing it to fruition.

I am grateful to Christine Chapman and her diligent and accurate transcribing of taped interviews that were not always recorded in the most conducive circumstances. Thanks also go to Bronwen Hanna and Michele Smart for editorial advice given with the frankness and honesty that possibly only comes from family! The book is much better for their efforts. I have been glad of Leigh Hatcher's enthusiasm in spurring me on and his assistance in pinning down an ever-allusive title. I very much appreciate the generosity of my current employers, John Dickson and Greg Clarke, for allowing me the time to complete the project.

Finally, and importantly, I offer sincere gratitude to each of the 13 subjects for generously allowing me some space in their busy lives and especially for entrusting something of their story to me. Their candour and openness allowed the discussion to move easily beyond the superficial and into the things of life that really matter. I hope I have managed to represent faithfully the conversations we had and honour the lives represented here.

Foreword

This is a remarkable collection of Australian stories – the senior policeman and the prisoner; the surgeon and the soldier; the sporting heroes.

Some are high profile like Tim Costello or hold leading positions like Federal Court Justice John Gilmour. Others, like the foster mother Carolyn Stedman, are largely unknown. We may recognise Leigh Hatcher from reading the news, but know little about his battle against a debilitating illness. And we may never have heard of Major Joyce Harmer if we did not have the chance to witness her love and grace in extraordinary circumstances.

These Australians have led strikingly varied lives. Justin Langer scores a century against England in the Boxing Day test. Bruce Robinson provides emergency care in Aceh following the Boxing Day tsunami. John Yeo takes the time to listen to his spinal patients facing pain and despair. Cameron Watt confesses his crime and heads to jail.

Despite these different life experiences, these Australians are men and women of faith. They believe there is an invisible architecture to this life, not always easy to explain or understand. As they have used their gifts and their skills, as they have faced hardship or failure, they speak with a sense of peace and purpose, confidence and conviction that is anchored in their Christian belief. It is a constant that gives them a sense of hope and understanding about the role they are to play in this world.

In the eleventh chapter of Hebrews, there is an honour roll of faith – a list of men and women who, by acts of faith, did remarkable things. Some names are famous, like Abraham, Moses and Joseph. The chapter also talks about the others who are not known by name, who did not achieve great fame and who endured hardship living lives of faith.

But for all of them: the big names and those we have never heard of, their faith 'was the firm foundation under everything that makes life worth living'.

It is the same with the stories here and that's what makes this book so interesting to read. These lives are so different. Some have been cheered by millions and have given speeches to vast crowds. Some have healed broken bodies; others have held battered babies. They have arrested murderers and comforted murderers. But they have all done so, believing and experiencing the transforming power of Jesus Christ in their own lives. At times, some people have viewed a confession of faith as a sign of weakness. These lives demonstrate the strength, courage and compassion that grow from faith.

Hearing these Australians talk frankly about their faith and their doubts, their convictions and their questions, is inspirational. We owe them thanks for sharing their stories and Simon Smart thanks for telling these stories so well.

Mark Scott

Managing Director, Australian Broadcasting Corporation

Introduction

'To be a person is to have a story to tell'
Isak Dineson

Stories have a way of getting under our skin. At their best, they are a powerful vehicle for expressing something at the heart of the human condition, something of our longings and fears, our hopes and dreams. Stories speak into the best parts of us, as well as the darkness. Through story we find a way of capturing moments of truth and beauty, heartbreak and wonder.

Every life is rich in drama. Personal narratives, if we scratch beneath the surface, can be especially powerful in illuminating life's deepest questions and struggles. This is no truer than in the area of faith. Where a sophisticated philosophical argument for God's existence might render us utterly unmoved, a personal story of a transformed life can capture our attention. It may be that a carefully constructed theological explanation of suffering leaves us cold, whereas one person's account of remarkable endurance disturbs our convictions, and stirs our imagination. There may be very little by way of evidence or proof in any of this, and yet, somehow within the authentic personal story we can sense we are touching something profound.

The following chapters recount the experience of faith of some remarkable people. They represent a wide variety of backgrounds, life experiences, ages and professions. There are two renowned doctors, a judge, two professional sportsmen, a television newsreader, a policeman, a former prisoner and his wife, a court chaplain, a soldier, the head of an aid organisation, and a mum to many. Common to them all is a deep conviction of faith in Jesus as the key to life and the source of hope. This of course places them somewhat out of sync with the dominant secular culture, even as they take their place firmly in it. Each case is an example of a true 'journey of faith' enduring at times profound challenges and struggles. A shared theme is optimism despite all that life can and does throw up at us, and the difference faith can make in a life.

Many of the subjects here are well known, highly accomplished and widely respected. I have tried to show how their belief in something beyond the material world has intersected with and contributed to their personal and professional lives, and why they have held on to faith over many years – in some cases, over a lifetime.

In his book, *The Longing for Home*, American author Frederick Buechner writes, 'No matter how much the world shatters us to pieces, we carry inside us a *vision* of wholeness that we sense is our true home and that beckons to us'. While none of the interviewees here would claim they have reached anything like complete wholeness, my sense is that they too have at least glimpsed what that might look like. As it beckons them, they follow.

It was a great privilege to sit with them and hear a small part of their story. I am grateful for their generosity in giving their time, and inviting me into their homes or places of work. I feel like I have been challenged and enlarged by the experience, and encouraged to live differently because of it. I offer these stories in the hope that they will do the same for those who read them; that something of the honesty and authentic nature of what was originally recounted will come through the pages. I found these people inspiring. I hope you do too.

'Christian faith is actually a protest against an order that says the powerful will always rip off the powerless, that greed will always win out.'

Costello

CEO World Vision Australia

Tim Costello claims that he is naturally a lazy person, but I don't believe him. I suggest as much, sitting in his office at World Vision Australia's headquarters in Melbourne – the location of the conversation alone being enough to put any such notion to rest. You don't get to be the CEO of an organisation of 400 staff with an annual budget of over $300 million by perfecting the art of procrastination. If, as Costello claims, his natural state essentially involves decomposing on the couch watching cricket or football, and that only by willpower does he manage to organise a lifestyle that keeps him busy and engaged, his must be a gargantuan will.

' ... the glass is always half full, not half empty with me. I see every enemy as a potential friend. I see every obstacle as something that won't stop me'.

This 53-year-old loafer has written several books, acted as a lawyer, been the mayor of St Kilda, the minister of two churches, the President of the Baptist Union, and Executive Director of *Urban Seed* – a service for the urban poor and homeless. Costello has tirelessly and passionately campaigned for welfare and social justice issues, and has been at the forefront of public debates on homelessness, gambling addiction, urban poverty and reconciliation. He was Victorian of the Year in 2004, and in 2005 was made an Officer of the Order of Australia. While younger brother Peter spent a decade crunching the numbers for the nation as the Federal Treasurer, Tim has crunched hearts, lobbied governments, pestered big business, and badgered complacent communities, all in the name of the poor, the ignored and the voiceless. Costello has clearly felt called into the areas of life that he says, 'break the heart of God: the growing gap between rich and poor, the crushing of hope of those who feel ... there is no stake for them in this society'.[1]

In recent years, Costello's dedication to the cause has brought him to the CEO's chair at World Vision where his focus has turned to international issues such as the *Make Poverty History* campaign, child sponsorship and micro development for the Third World. In this capacity, he has rubbed shoulders with Irish rocker Bono from U2 – the men appear an unlikely duo in many respects – until you realise how much they share. Both exude a burning and righteous anger at the worst of the globe's injustices. They each seem to positively bounce with optimism that something really can be done to solve the problems, and will incessantly remind us all that 30 000 children a day die due to extreme and avoidable poverty – a statistic we can never seem to hear enough times to make us comfortable.

I ask Costello whether he is a pragmatist or a romantic and which is better suited to running an aid agency. 'I'm an utter romantic, but a pragmatist is much more suited to running an organisation like World Vision', he smiles. '[Between those extremes] there is the tension and 'mind the gap'. I am incurably optimistic, and the glass is always half full, not half empty with me. I see every enemy as a potential friend. I see every obstacle as something that won't stop me.' While he acknowledges deep disappointment and hurt when barriers have proven immovable, and enemies have not been won over, he says 'it hasn't altered my DNA which is a romantic'. Such a quality is vital for the

---

1. *A conversation with Tim Costello*, Compass ABC TV
   www.abc.net.au/compass/s356569.htm accessed 2/4/07

area of work Costello is involved in – setting the vision and drawing others along with him. A team of managers siphoning his idealistic plans through a filter of pragmatism produces an outcome that Costello says is 'realistic, but also full of hope'.

Like all good leaders, Costello has a presence, that indefinable magnetic quality that demands attention. Fiona McLeay, General Counsel for World Vision, says of her boss, 'He's got the capacity to put his finger on the mood of the moment, so he can really sense trends and directions and what's going to inspire people'. She remembers fondly his address to a large crowd gathered for the *Make Poverty History* concert in Melbourne in late 2006, a five-minute talk she feels electrified the whole event.

In his various roles Costello has commanded the type of media exposure that would be the envy of many politicians. He stands at an imposing height, (my guess is about 6ft 3in) and speaks with a deep, resonant tone equally suited to pulpit, radio or TV studio. Costello has shone in all three places. For someone whose life is so full and schedule so demanding, he is remarkably relaxed; a quality that he says has given him longevity in a game rife with burnout. On the day I spoke with him, he managed to slot me in-between team meetings and a television interview. Two days later he was travelling to Darfur in Western Sudan.

Clearly a man of passion, where did Costello get his heart for social justice? Growing up on Main St. Blackburn, an outer suburb of Melbourne in a humble three-bedroom weatherboard house, the eldest son of two teachers, Costello says his formative years were stable. He, along with Peter and their sister Janet, enjoyed a strong family life surrounded by a network of good neighbours and church friends. Theirs was a typical suburban existence in the 1960s, conservative and uncomplicated, and Costello says life revolved around church, school and sport. Unlike Peter, who was dedicated and diligent, Tim preferred sport and other distractions. 'I think I was the only teacher's son at Carey [Baptist Grammar] who never became a prefect', he laughs, admitting that this failure is hardly emblematic of a wayward youth. 'Yeah, I mucked around a bit – not really bad, but a bit.' The Costello home was one of stimulating debate; a laboratory of learning where history and politics were given prominence along with an 'engagement with life, and interest in what was happening in the world', he says. It was thus a natural progression when both Costello boys ended up studying Law at Monash University.

'He would come in and say, "I don't care who's right and wrong, I'm going to belt you both"', laughs Costello, admitting he probably deserved the treatment 90% of the time ...

Costello points to the Baptist church environment that he grew up in as a crucial shaping influence in the work he would take on as an adult. 'The heroic people in my childhood were essentially the missionaries who had gone to build a school; be a medical doctor; be a person caring for others', he explains. When I suggest that most normal children do not respond to visiting missionaries in quite the same way, but rather draw their inspiration from rock stars, big screen actors and sporting legends, Costello volunteers that while he had his heroes at the Essendon football club, he never 'mistook them as heroes in a moral sense'. I refrain from admitting just how old I was before realising the cricket and football stars of my childhood weren't also saints.

Along with the Baptists, his father's approach to corporal punishment laid important foundations in being attuned to justice issues. 'He would come in and say, "I don't care who's right and wrong, I'm going to belt you both"', laughs Costello, admitting he probably deserved the treatment 90% of the time he and his brother were on the receiving end of the strap. 'I remember thinking "that just isn't fair, he *should* be concerned who's right and wrong".'

'Uranium mining you have to think about, I mean, is it moral to put a toxic, feral product in the ground for 250 000 years, if the earth is the Lord's?'

Whatever were the most important formative influences on Costello he has always married deep commitment to his Christian faith with a heart for others. 'I believe "sin" is all that cripples the image of God [within people]', he explains. 'Salvation is *all* that restores that image that's been crippled – so it is the news that God loves you and sent his son to die for you, and it is clean water and access to food that restores that. World Vision aims to address the brokenness of people in a world where the church has given up on that brokenness – but God hasn't given up.'

Frederick Buechner once wrote that God calls us to the place that intersects our greatest passion with the greatest need. Costello has clearly felt the force of that intersection. 'Look, I have felt it a number of times', he says, describing memorable preaching moments along with the successful campaign to reduce the proposed number of poker machines of the Kennett-led Victorian Liberal government from 90 000 to 25 000. 'I felt great exhilaration and passion intersecting with the need to stop the spread of a highly addictive machine that was ruthlessly transferring money from the poorest people in our city to the richest, the captains of the gaming industry. I felt those moments time and again in World Vision where people who in the lottery of life had no chance – they were just born on the wrong latitude, without clean water, universal health, enough food – have been given a chance to fulfil their God-given potential. That has been very moving.'

Costello is enamoured with the power of stories to convey powerful messages and I ask him about the narratives that have impacted him. He recounts a story his father told him about a man – yet another missionary – who in the 1940s, after burying his wife and son on the mission field returned home on a boat to face a crowded dock with not a single person there to greet him. Crying out to God in bitterness about his loss and lack of welcome, he sensed God telling him, 'Son, you are not home yet'. The story had a profound impact on the young Costello. 'If you really believe in the resurrection, it frees you to take risks now. You do not have to have every experience, every pay rise and career promotion and squeeze everything into this one life. There is another life, and you can live vulnerably, sacrificially. I understood that belief in the resurrection and heaven wasn't just a sort of comfortable notion, but rather, it actually disturbs the present and calls you to live out discipleship here and now.'

I have heard political commentators say that they would like to be a fly on the wall in the Costello family home over Christmas lunch – a reference to the perceived chasm between the politics of the two brothers. On the question of faith and politics, Tim Costello's response is considered and emphatic. 'My faith determines everything, from marriage to community to worldview to politics. Having said that, the institutional expressions of politics need to be separated. Absolutely think about who you're going to vote for in the light of what the Kingdom of God would say about these issues – you know global warming is an issue because the earth is the Lord's and we are stewards. Uranium mining you have to think about, I mean, is it moral to put a toxic, feral product in the ground for 250 000 years, if the earth is the Lord's? You have to think about what the Kingdom of God would have to say about those who are the least – the strangers who in our context are migrants and boatpeople – so faith must inform politics. But then you don't want a Christian party saying this is the Christian position. You want Christians in all parties.'

Costello is clearly someone who has not been broken by life despite witnessing some of the worst that both humanity and nature can dish out. In 2004 when the Boxing Day tsunami wiped out over 200 000 people, he was on the ground in the disaster zone in Sri Lanka only 40 hours after the wave tore through the countryside destroying everything in its path. 'During the tsunami I was in great despair', he says. 'There were apocalyptic scenes with bodies everywhere, particularly kids. There were people standing there staring out to sea hoping against hope that someone was coming – being washed back alive – and at that point you say to yourself, "Where is God?" That's the question you ask, "Where is God?"' Since we spoke Costello has had to face similar experiences in Burma following the 2008 cyclone.

Costello admits that during the dark days of the tsunami he was pushed to the very limits of his faith. There are impenetrable questions that he knows could be answered only by God himself, and yet he hangs on. 'I'd still rather be here with my faith and my questions than abandoning my faith or having trite answers', he explains.

And he believes there are good reasons for hope. The response of the Australian public to the tsunami – an overwhelming outpouring of generosity – led Costello to describe the period as 'the best of times and the worst of times'.

Referring to his work for World Vision, he says, 'greed, abuse of power and human malevolence account for a lot of suffering and I'm exposed to that on every trip I go on'. But alongside what he calls the fundamental fracture that runs through all of us, he also clearly sees potential for redemption. 'That's what I appeal to, preach to for a change of heart and believe is the dominant thing in my work rather than the rawness of human evil, which I see plenty of too.'

'There were people standing there staring out to sea hoping against hope that someone was coming – being washed back alive – and at that point you say to yourself, "Where is God?"'

'Christian faith is actually a protest against an order that says the powerful will always rip off the powerless, that greed will always win out. My Christian faith says that God has shown his face in Jesus who as a Jew stands in the Exodus tradition where slaves are set free and the widow, the orphan and the stranger are cared for. The Kingdom of God at its heart, preached by Jesus in the Gospels of Matthew, Mark and Luke, is good news for the poor. ...So my faith says that God *is* engaged in the struggle against all that cripples, all that causes suffering. God is fundamentally engaged in that struggle in the person of Jesus and that gives me great hope; that all this isn't simply a forlorn protest by me, it is fundamental to the work God is doing in the world.'

While God might be working in the world, Costello admits the Creator has a hard time being heard in the West. 'Yes, I think Western culture is the most resistant to the Gospel and spiritual dimension, of any culture that we have seen, because it is utterly self-sufficient; it's confident about its ability to solve problems; to create an ever-increasing range of consumerist experiences and goods.' Costello believes the never-ending line of material goods that entertain and distract; dulling the pain while trivialising life, make it very difficult to talk about the transformative dimension of Christian faith. 'It makes more sense in Africa and Asia where I visit regularly now.'

'More and more people are asking, "How is it possible when we have solved the problem of supply that there is an epidemic of depression?"'

Ironically Costello sees the hope for the West in its ultimate failure to deliver a meaningful life. 'More and more people are asking, "How is it possible when we have solved the problem of supply that there is an epidemic of depression?" ... There's got to be something that grounds happiness rather than ever-increasing prosperity – the wealth to happiness story that dominates our society.'

At a more personal level, Costello, like every believer, faces the challenge of living up to his calling of following Jesus, and it isn't easy. As something of a celebrity in the world he inhabits,

Costello knows there are people who have him on a pedestal. 'The danger is ... the gap between who you really are and what people perceive', he says. On that front his family serve a vital function. 'Wives smell bull a mile off', he adds emphatically. Fiona McLeay says of her interaction with Costello, 'I think one of the good things about working closely with him is you see that he is very human, so it is not as if he is some kind of mythical figure who can do anything. ... He's very real and he's the first to admit that as well, which of course makes him more inspiring, not less'.

German theologian Dietrich Bonhoeffer, of whom Costello is a fan, once said, 'Mere waiting and looking is not Christian behaviour. ... Christians are called to sympathy and action'. Costello has had his critics in the church. There are those who fear his campaigning for issues of justice and poverty takes precedence over a proclamation of the Gospel. For Tim Costello, however, it is impossible to separate the two. To declare the message of hope without accompanying activism would have a hollow ring to it and ultimately betray the message. Getting in on what the Kingdom of God is about, he feels, is too important an opportunity to miss. It's what inspires and motivates him. It's what gets him up off the couch, or away from the tennis court; it's what drives him to boardrooms, university halls, politician's offices, churches, schools and Third World orphanages. Costello is in a fight, perhaps against his own leanings towards indolence, certainly against poverty and injustice. Countless people stand to benefit while ever he can maintain the rage, and he doesn't look like slowing down any time soon.

Assoc

'I know that God is real despite all the wretchedness.'

te Professor
John Yeo

Spinal Specialist

When I was very young – perhaps nine or ten, I saw a movie based on the true-life story of Jill Kinmont who, as an 18-year-old, broke her neck in a skiing accident. She became a quadriplegic and the film tracked her struggle to construct a life from her shattered dreams and broken body. As if all that wasn't bad enough, there were failed relationships, and the ultimate dagger to the heart, when the love of her life was killed in a light plane crash on his way to their wedding.

It was probably a really bad film. Reviews I recently unearthed suggest as much. But as a kid I was profoundly impacted by the tragedy of it all – especially her injuries. I guess even at that age I had grasped something of the crashing devastation of a healthy, vibrant body being broken; a zestful, young life torn apart; the permanence. In a sense the horror of it never left me.

For well over 40 years, Professor John Yeo has gone to work each day and faced that same story, repeated in various forms over and over again. He has been involved in the care of over 3000 paraplegic and quadriplegic (the preferred term these days is tetraplegic) casualties in his career as a specialist in spinal injury care.[2] For decades he has sat with, nursed, operated on, cajoled, counselled, and lobbied on behalf of those facing the finality of spinal cord damage. He has spent a lifetime fighting to make things better for those who have been left, by a cruel twist of fate, completely and permanently immobile. The chances are, if you had a spinal injury in NSW after 1964, you may well have come across Professor Yeo. Many readers will thus be glad they don't know him.

It would be difficult to measure Yeo's influence, but those who are engaged in spinal work will tell you of his integral role in revolutionizing the care of spinal patients, in rehabilitation and, importantly, in the prevention of injuries. In 1982 Yeo was awarded the Order of Australia, and in 2000, the Annual Medal from the International Spinal Cord Society. A fellow of the Royal Australasian College of Surgeons, and the Royal Australasian

---

2. Lise Mellor, *150 years, 150 firsts – the people of the Faculty of Medicine,* University of Sydney, (Sydney University Press, 2006), pages 56 – 57.

College of Physicians (Faculty of Rehabilitation Medicine), he has been a lecturer, expert medico legal consultant, advisor, and is in demand around the world to treat and offer advice in the care and prevention of spinal injuries.

... the Headmaster at North Sydney Boys' High declared, 'Yeo, you will never succeed in medicine'.

I have known John for many years through family connections and have always liked him. His self-deprecating humour and generous nature accompany a rare ability to make whomever he is speaking with feel significant – to make them feel like they matter. If, as a friend of mine says, the mark of a truly great person is the way they treat the 'little' people, then John Yeo surely qualifies.

I wonder whether the empathy and humility that he is well known for, come in part from a life where nothing was handed to him, and in which he had to endure significant setbacks, twists and turns on the road to what he now sees as his medical calling. Indeed that journey involved a circuitous route for the young and ambitious would-be surgeon, beginning in the 1950s when the Headmaster at North Sydney Boys' High declared, 'Yeo, you will never succeed in medicine'. (Is it just me or was this type of advice straight out of the pages of the teacher's handbook of that era?) Notwithstanding that inspiration, a Commonwealth scholarship and strong parental support enabled him to study at Sydney University – the clinical years at North Shore Hospital confirming in Yeo's mind that he was in the right game. He enjoyed his interaction with the patients.

Yeo had a fight on his hands.
First he had to convince patients and
their families that life was worth living.

Next stop was England in 1958, and the Royal College of Surgeons. He spent six weeks at sea as a ship's doctor with a crew of 40, all hailing from Liverpool in England. 'They were the toughest group of men I'd ever met', says John. 'I learnt a few phrases and concepts I'd never heard of before', he laughs. These were challenging and exhilarating times. On arrival in London, Yeo admits he got caught up in the excitement of the big city where he was exposed to a whole new world and became distracted from the main task. Subsequently his first attempt at the surgeon's exam was unsuccessful. With no money left, Yeo was forced back to hospital work. A year at Shoreham-by-sea, Sussex, as registrar in Southlands Hospital gave him experience in orthopaedics and urology, and instruction by some excellent surgeons.

Yeo next moved to Saskatchewan in Canada and endured the biting winter of minus 40 degrees Celsius while working in General Practice. Again he gained what would eventually become vitally significant medical experiences. Yet at the time John felt about as far from his goal of being a surgeon as he could get.

He now sees God's hand in those struggles. 'At times I thought, "What a mess all this is", and "How on earth are you going to see purpose in all that, John?"' he says. 'But I think this is where you feel God is overseeing what happens, and you are just thankful that you are part of that plan ... and it was a case of doors closing and doors opening, and I think the rest of my life has been that way. It seems haphazard, but there is a plan and there is a reason – someone's opening those doors and someone's closing them', John says. No experience was wasted. He can now see that the skills and experiences he acquired in England, Canada and elsewhere were vital ingredients in preparing him for the defining role of his life as Director of the Spinal Injuries Unit at Sydney's Royal North Shore Hospital, where he was appointed in 1968.

While his title might have had a nice ring to it, at the time it was hardly the bright lights and prestige of medical celebrity. In fact, it involved eating 'a fair amount of humble pie', says John, of the early years at the unit. What is now a world-class facility was, in those days, a fibro cottage on the fringe of the hospital grounds, with 11 paralysed patients literally facing the wall without hope. Life expectancy for the paralysed was very low back then. A nursing colleague of John's remembers helping patients to endure mid-summer sweltering heat in the cottages, by taking them onto the lawn on mattresses and hosing them down with a garden hose. After a newspaper ran this as a feature on the front page, air-conditioning was soon installed! In those early years, Yeo acted not only as director, but on occasion wardsman, nurse and even bus driver when taking patients on excursions.

Yeo had a fight on his hands. First he had to convince patients and their families that life was worth living. He had to take the battle for beds, facilities and access for paralysed people to the world of the able-bodied, to hospital administration, to governments and to the community. All of this required a bit of 'fire in the belly', as he puts it. The International Year of the Disabled in 1981 was something of a breakthrough that John says 'helped to give a new vision to the community that the disabled were people to be reckoned with'. Meanwhile Yeo was ramping up the care for his patients. The team around him included a neurosurgeon, orthopaedic surgeon, urologist, a plastic surgeon, experts in nursing care, physiotherapists, occupational therapists, social workers, hospital chaplains, and of course intensive care facilities for the patients when they first came in. Yeo rolled up his sleeves and lobbied authorities to make inroads into patient care and community understanding.

Nancy Joyce, Yeo's senior nursing sister at the spinal unit for over 20 years, says it was the way Yeo treated people that marked him out as unique.

The desire to find a cure for spinal cord injury also drove Yeo into the laboratory for many years. What he sought was some reversibility to the damaged spinal cord. Using hyperbaric oxygen, Yeo was able to achieve improvement in the damaged nerves of sheep, which he used as the experimental model. The same concept was used on humans, but not before Yeo entered the hyperbaric chamber himself – unwilling to submit his patients to anything he wouldn't go through. Yeo didn't quite get the answers he was looking for, but in demonstrating some reversibility his efforts provided impetus for further research, which these days is making exciting progress using such techniques as adult stem cells placed in the injured spinal cord. All of this is painstaking work, and Yeo has played his part in what he says is a long haul, and very much a team approach.

In 1972, Annette Jamison was only 19 years old when she dived into an ocean pool and broke her neck. She became a tetraplegic through her injury and spent nine months under John Yeo's care in the unit at North Shore. According to Annette, it was John's warmth, humour and ability to bring comfort not only to the patients but also to their families, which made him unique. 'I can't sing his praises highly enough', she says and believes many other patients share her feelings. 'They still speak of him so glowingly. There was a wonderful confidence that John was able to engender in his patients.'

'John's approach to all the things he does is very much with Christ in mind', Annette adds. 'It makes him the man of integrity that he is. Everyone who knows him would attest to that. I don't know that I've ever seen him lose his block, and I was there every day for nine months and seeing him on a daily basis. The only areas that he would get angry about would be somebody not doing their job in taking care of one of his patients ... he would not tolerate incompetence. In many ways it was those high standards that have left me with the legacy of being convinced that I could do anything', says Annette.

Nancy Joyce, Yeo's senior nursing sister at the spinal unit for over 20 years, says it was the way Yeo treated people that marked him out as unique. She speaks of his patience, kindness, and understanding nature – something she admits not all doctors of Yeo's standing possess. 'He always had time to listen', she says. 'People felt comfortable with him ... people felt valued. He just showed so much care and compassion, and that never changed.'

Perhaps still fixated on my movie experiences as a boy, I ask John about the early stages when an injured patient first arrives at the hospital. '[It] would be a tremendous challenge to see this patient brought into casualty, lying immobile with eyes wide open and fearful. Often people were conscious and aware that they were in terrible trouble because they couldn't move their arms or legs; they were having difficulty breathing, they couldn't pass any urine – they realised that their body was in great difficulty. And so often they were in the prime of life – late adolescence, early 20s, you know whatever age it is, it is an enormous challenge to suddenly realise what you are facing', says John.

While just a handful of patients would get almost full recovery the vast majority would be left with 'profound loss of motor power and feeling'. John is clearly not impervious to the tragedy of it all; despite the number of times he has seen it. 'That doesn't stop you from shedding a few tears because you know when the patient first comes in, and it's a father or mother, you know, newly married, or with a couple of young children. On the balance of probabilities, having a look at the x-rays and seeing the damage to the spinal cord in the operating theatre, you know that this person is going to be in a wheelchair forever. And then you envisage the patient wheeling down the corridor with those one or two little children on the footplates of a wheelchair, and maybe that's as close as they're going to get to share fun with the kids! That always gets to you', he says.

Breaking grim news to patients and their families was never easy. 'We'd say, "Well, we are going to get the bones back and stabilise the spine and then we are going to have to wait and see whether the bruised spinal cord is going to recover. I cannot promise you that it will, but we can be hopeful". And they sometimes would say, "We believe in miracles, Doctor", and I'd say, "Yes, I believe in miracles too but it may not be the miracle that you are thinking of". So, to be honest, the miracle for most people in the spinal unit is that they will go back to being first-class citizens, in a wheelchair.'

John's Christian faith has endured daily contact with profound sorrow, struggle and suffering. I am interested in the interplay between what John has dealt with in his professional life and his long held beliefs. He admits that the confronting nature of these dire moments raises spiritual questions for him. '"Where is God in all this?" is the question that still comes up for me', he says, but adds that he has learned a great deal about the purpose of life by participating in the struggle alongside his disabled patients.

He was first introduced to Christianity at primary school. 'I do remember that lovely Scripture teacher who said, "Well you should become a Christian and the way to do that is to take home this little booklet and sign the bottom line here and that will make you a Christian"', smiles John. 'Well it didn't of course. I think I signed it a few times and still wasn't sure if I was headed to the party or not, but it was a starting point.'

He admits that the confronting nature of these dire moments raises spiritual questions for him. '"Where is God in all this?" is the question that still comes up for me.'

That starting point blossomed into a stronger commitment and involvement in Christian groups at high school, teaching Sunday school and at university in the 1950s, being involved in big missions like the Billy Graham Crusade. 'In the university days we thought we knew everything', admits John. 'We knew every problem that people were likely to face', he says with a wry smile.

John avoids neat answers when discussing the way he processes the question of faith and suffering. I once heard him say that he felt that 80% of the pain is borne by 20% of the population, so I ask him about that. 'When I come to ask why does this tremendous hurt occur often in a repetitive way, not because of a single event or tragedy but multiple events, I don't understand that, and there is no way a human being can understand that entirely', he says.

'I know it is God who has helped me to be involved in this complex, challenging and sad situation with all its moments of being uplifted by achievement, courage and endurance and by what people do despite their disabilities.'

Yet John's sense of perspective and knowledge of the potential for good to emerge from great pain and tragedy are very real. 'I've admired people who have continued to grow despite the enormous difficulties, both physical and psychological, and the difficulties with the journey of faith', he says. 'So many people have said, "You know it's a funny thing, you'll think I'm strange saying this, but I have really found something in life that I don't think I would have found had this tragedy not occurred"', recounts John. Importantly he wants me to know that 'They've said that, not me'. This is anything but head-in-the-sand optimism and John is quick to acknowledge that not all people make it. Indeed he has been close at hand to see a number of people who couldn't cope and lost the will to live. Mostly these are patients who have no-one to share their journey.

A strong thread through John's thought is the critical importance of sharing the journey of life with others – the love and support of friends, family and community. It is what he has seen as the vital ingredient in the life of spinal patients. The same applies to issues of faith for John. 'The only way I can reconcile my personal knowledge of a loving God – not just the loving God as revealed through Christ for me, although that's the cornerstone of my faith, but a loving God who has revealed that love today, beyond the resurrection – is to see the purposes of God in what's happening today. One of the ways that I've been able to see the reality of the loving God, here in this century, in this age, in this city, in this suburb, in North Shore Hospital with all of that challenge, is that I see God reflected in people around me ... I see the importance of the group, or the family or the tribe, rather than necessarily just the individual. To me ... the importance of faith is knowing that God is working through you and me, warts and all, and because of that I know that God is real, despite all the wretchedness.'

'C.S. Lewis, if I translate him correctly, suggests that "heaven is the place where you enjoy passing the ball". That summarises for me, I think, what this is all about – it is sharing this journey, it is a family approach, it is the neighbourly thing to do. It's also realising the responsibility that if my next-door neighbour says, "I don't see God in you", then I'm responsible ... that's an awesome thing to remember.'

'Do we walk out there every day, or wheel out there every day and someone says as they say in that famous film, "I'll have what she's having"', laughs John. Commenting on John's faith, Nancy Joyce says, 'He just lives it out'.

Of his life in spinal injury care John offers this summary. 'I know it is God who has helped me to be involved in this complex, challenging and sad situation with all its moments of being uplifted by achievement, courage and endurance and by what people do despite their disabilities.'

It is no real surprise that John Yeo likes to talk about C.S. Lewis' book on suffering, *The Problem of Pain*, because it deals with a theological issue that John has clearly been forced to wrestle with. In closing this chapter I quote Lewis from the preface to that work. When I read it, I hear John's voice:

For the ... task of teaching fortitude and patience I was never fool enough to suppose myself qualified, nor have I anything to offer my readers except my conviction that when pain is to be borne, a little courage helps more than knowledge, a little human sympathy more than much courage, and the least tincture of the love of God more than all.

'How do you love someone a little bit? For me it's all or nothing.'

Carol

Stedman

Foster Mother

I once lived two floors above a single mother who was a heroin addict. Somewhere in a distant past, life had gone wrong for her and she was now a prisoner of her addiction, utterly unable to function without ruinous chemicals flowing through her veins. Her life revolved around prostitution, theft, multiple partners, and the agonising space between hits. To varying degrees, every one of her neighbours experienced that agony. She was monstrously violent, manipulative, dishonest, and self-obsessed. The intensity of her screaming, howling and glass-breaking fury was confronting enough as an adult secure above the carnage, but that two small boys huddled in the corner of her apartment, was truly intolerable. All of us in the street made weekly calls to the police in the middle of the night. Many of us sat on hold to Community Services begging them to rescue the children.

The trauma these boys were exposed to can only have done untold long-term damage. It's probably too much to hope that when they were finally removed from their mother, they were delivered into the care of someone like Carolyn Stedman. If they were, perhaps there is some hope for them.

More than 30 years ago, Carolyn Stedman, at that stage a mother of two girls aged five and three, heard a radio interview about the desperate need for foster carers. Scrawling down a number, she spoke that night to her husband David, and before long the two of them were enrolled in a 10-week course with The Department of Community Services (DOCS). Placed on a list of short and medium length carers, they were soon to take in their first foster child, a five-year-old with an alcoholic mother. In the intervening years, Carolyn has raised six of her own children, run a family home day-care centre, and been a foster mum to over 60 children. Each foster kid has been special to her. There isn't one who didn't break her heart one way or another.

Sitting opposite Carolyn in her lounge room, I am immediately struck by the orderliness that surrounds me. It's a well-worn home that grew rooms as more children appeared over the years, but there is not a thing out of place and it is frighteningly clean. I can picture the large central dining area, silent and empty today, full of conversation, laughter, bickering, fights, food, competition, tears and love, as all large families experience. It's sleep time for the day-care kids, and I think I counted five prams lined against the wall with military precision, each flanked with a child's backpack and shoes. This is a no-nonsense home, but one that oozes lived-in family warmth and familiarity. Photographs surround the walls of children at various ages and stages of fashion crime and teenage awkwardness. Not surprisingly, it is not only the blood members of the family in these pictures, but many foster kids as well.

Each foster kid has been special to her. There isn't one who didn't break her heart one way or another.

Carolyn is a straightforward self-effacing grandmother of 13, with an extraordinary story to tell. When she accepted that first child into her home on Sydney's privileged North Shore, she was probably not prepared for the contact with dire abuse, drug and alcohol addiction, prostitution, mental illness and violence that she would (indirectly) experience over the years. As she acknowledges, there are some kids who are fostered for reasons that are relatively benign but not many. Carolyn and David volunteered to take children in crisis situations when the need arose.

As they soon found out, the need was great. Some of the stories Carolyn tells are agonising; the sort you quickly want to consign to your subconscious. 'We've had babies who were victims of violence. One child had two broken legs and one broken arm. He was very hard to bath, that poor little fellow', says Carolyn. 'We've had children who have come and haven't had a nappy change for weeks and weeks. So you have to put them in a bath and soak it off, and then a layer of skin comes off with it; children who haven't had anything to eat for days, absolutely starving.'

' ... His parents were both drug addicts. He came with a fractured skull when he was about two weeks old. They said he climbed out of a pram. Most two-week-old babies don't climb out of prams.'

'We had another little boy, who was with us for more than a year. His parents were both drug addicts. He came with a fractured skull when he was about two weeks old. They said he climbed out of a pram. Most two-week-old babies don't climb out of prams, or even roll out of prams. Anyway, as time went on, the department was trying to restore him to his parents, and so they got them government housing, a fridge, a second-hand car so that they could go and get their methadone. They gave them a cot and linen, everything you need for a small child. They got them all set up and then started having visits. So he'd be picked up from me and would go and visit for a couple of hours with a social worker sitting by to make sure things were going well. Then they started doing it for a full day instead of a couple of hours, and then the social worker dropped him off and didn't stay. So gradually the parents were given responsibility. I kept saying, "He smells of marijuana every time he comes home". I'm sure he hadn't been fed. Certainly his clothes hadn't been changed; he was still in the same nappy because I marked a few of them with red texta so I'd know if he'd been changed. No, he was still in the same nappy when he got home. Anyway, eventually he was doing overnights, coming home an absolute mess. He'd be terribly distressed when he got back. He was dirty and he hadn't been fed. But anyway the end of the story for him was he was returned [to his parents], and he was found caged about a month later. So he was then removed and went into long-term care. They're the sorts of outcomes that I hear about. I was so upset about that. I still am. The parents were still using drugs; there's absolutely no doubt about that, but the system allowed him to go back.'

Carolyn has a deep concern about a system that gives parents too many chances. And she ought to know. The story of twins – a boy and a girl – who came to her three times, spells this out. 'Our family absolutely loved those twins', says Carolyn. 'Their mother was an alcoholic. The babies had been found in a home unit in baskets when they were only a couple of weeks old. A boatload of American sailors had come into town and she'd disappeared leaving a 14-month-old and the twins. The neighbours had reported crying; when they were picked up by the department, the 14-month-old was sitting between the two bassinettes on the floor patting the babies on their backs. And that is the story of dysfunctional families when parents are drug addicts. Their children take over the role of the carer. First, they were taken to the hospital to be re-hydrated. So after that, the grandmother took the 14-month-old and the twins came here.

So the whole thing went to court after a few months and for the court appearance mum got herself sober, put on a suit, got her hair cut, got done up and the magistrate said, "Everything looks OK", and back they went.'

The twins returned to Carolyn three times, but by the fourth time, the Stedmans had other foster kids and couldn't take them in. 'They were then sent off to some other people they didn't know, and in a way I feel I have been a part of the further damaging of children, just through being part of the system', says Carolyn.

She is however very quick to defend DOCS and the workers there, who are hopelessly overworked and under-resourced. Carolyn insists that it is not the DOCS workers who are to blame for the many faults in the system, but a society that places too little value on its most precious and vulnerable asset – its children.

So how does Carolyn find such an enormous capacity to care? It's hard enough to continually drag yourself out of bed in the middle of the night for your own kids, let alone volunteer to do it for decades for someone else's. Her answer is simple. 'There's a real need there and somebody's got to do it.' And it gives her great satisfaction. Quite simply, she loves kids. Their innocence she finds beautiful; the spontaneity and the joy they bring with them becomes her joy. 'I found mothering, and parenting easy', she says. 'It's not hard for me. My friends now say to me, "How can you bare to have kids around you all day?" I love it, and I've come to realise that having the ability to care is a God-given gift. It's what I enjoy, it's what I'm good at.'

Carolyn articulates straightforward links between her commitment to all the children in her life, and her faith. 'I know there's a lot of Bible verses that require us to care for children, and because I know I'm a good carer, I am doing what God wants me to do; I strongly believe that. So that is my greatest motivation', she says. When pressed to express the questions she might have for God regarding the circumstances of the children she has cared for, her answers reflect a faith that is simple, but not simplistic. She clearly has had to face the darkness. 'When I think to myself, "Please don't let this child be restored to its drug addicted parents", and it sometimes is, I do ask "Why?" I just know that God is in control and I have to trust him and I do trust him. Even when the decision seems terrible to me, he knows much better than I do. He knows what he's doing on a much grander scale. So that's how I can sit with a baby going into a placement that I wouldn't have particularly chosen, and that has happened a number of times.'

'I love it, and I've come to realise that having the ability to care is a God-given gift. It's what I enjoy, it's what I'm good at.'

Whatever trust Carolyn has had in God, she in no sense pretends this has sheltered her from the pain of all that's involved in this business of foster care. Especially hard is letting them go. 'Eighteen months ago, I said goodbye to a little two-year-old girl called Amy.* On the morning she was to go I said to her in my most cheerful voice, "Amy, you are going to go and live with Lisa and Mike and you won't be coming back to Carolyn's house for a long, long time". And she was on my knee and she grabbed around my neck and sort of put her head on my shoulder and snuggled in and she was saying to me, "Don't do this to me". Anyway, at 10 o'clock, as arranged, Lisa arrived. This is the new foster mum, the long-term carer. But on the morning when I said

* Names of the people in each case have been changed to protect their identities.

to her, "Lisa is going to come and take you to her house and you won't be coming back to Carolyn's", she'd already had her second birthday here. She knew. She knew when I was telling her all this. And then there came the ring at the doorbell and she was wrapped around me – I had to peel her off me and get her into the car. She was crying. Oh dear! It's traumatic and it's hard for the whole family. It's not just me who's heartbroken, we're all crying.'

'There've been other times when children have been picked up and the whole family's been here and we have all come inside and burst into tears. We've waved the car off and there's this child looking out the car window at us. It's terrible. This is their world. This is all they know. The [goodbyes] get worse. You hear all your life that if you practise something, you'll get good at it. Not this; you practise it thousands of times, it gets worse every time.'

Carolyn has been on an emotional marathon that appears to have no end. When I ask her how she has survived, she quietly owns up to a quality that is as apparent as it is necessary to live the way she has. 'I am a strong person', she admits. 'A lot of people have said that to me over the years. A few people have also said, "It must be fun having foster children, but I suppose you must only love them a little bit because it must be hard to let them go". How do you do that? How do you love someone a little bit? For me it's all or nothing. It's not good for a child to love them a little bit, and I don't think it's possible anyway. It's not possible for me.'

Carolyn holds out hope that what she gives to the babies in her care is not in vain. 'I think to myself, maybe, somewhere deep down in their psyche they'll remember those first two years of their life and think, "I was loved, cuddled, caressed, kissed, tickled and had fun, you know, and I always felt secure and happy". When they've been with me from birth to two years they won't remember that, but there might be something there that stands them in good stead for forming long-term relationships later on. That sort of thing', explains Carolyn.

According to Carolyn, the personal gains and those of her family have outweighed the costs. Understandably, the Stedman kids at times resented the extra children vying for attention in an already busy household. Occasionally the foster children were very difficult, including one older boy who was aggressive and threatening. 'He was a most difficult, distressed, rejected, awful little boy. Such a sad case', says Carolyn.

'You hear all your life that if you practise something, you'll get good at it. Not this; you practise it thousands of times, it gets worse every time'.

The youngest of the Stedman clan, Cate, reflecting on her growing up says, 'Sometimes it was extremely difficult – kids were really badly behaved, or drug addicts, and put a lot of stress on Mum and Dad trying to deal with them, but in the long term it's been amazing. We grew up on the North Shore. We were a wealthy family. We would never have had to come into contact with people like this. It just made me so aware of what's out there and the horrible stuff that goes on in life', she says.

Reflecting on the years of fostering, Carolyn and David share a common sense of the ridiculous – a kind of collective resigned shrug and necessary macabre humour to accompany engagement with humanity gone awry: a prostitute prone to bringing enormous stuffed toys on every visit to her daughter living at the Stedman house (the same woman coming to dinner and leaving a cab waiting outside for three hours!); the baby boy, who at the first change of nappy, proved to be a girl. Then there was a two-year-old girl who explained to the whole family how to shoot up, using a child's medical kit. Whenever she would hear a siren she would hide, shouting, "That's the cops".

'It's been a lovely thing to do even though there's grief', says Carolyn. 'I don't actually see grief as a negative emotion ... It's an important part of life to be able to grieve.'

There have been many rewarding experiences. A girl whose mother had died when she was a baby was taken in by Carolyn and then adopted into a functioning, caring family. Her adoptive parents brought her back to the Stedmans when she was 12 years old to help her fill in the gaps of the first two years of her life. The reunion was an emotional one. 'That part of her life was missing', says Carolyn. 'So we got copies of the 14 photographs we had of her when she was one month old, two months old and what have you. She wanted to see the room where she slept, where she played and what toys she played with; and let me tell you, I still have most of the toys. That was a lovely, lovely experience. So there have been lots of highs.'

Then there was Gus, abandoned by his schizophrenic mother at birth. Gus's dad, a bricklayer from Alice Springs, had no idea of his existence until a phone call from DOCS informed him of the possibility that he was a father. 'He said he nearly fell through the floor', says Carolyn. 'They did a DNA test, and sure enough it all matched up beautifully. And so he came and stayed in Sydney for three days and came here each day to be taught how to parent. He was ... he was rough', says Carolyn searching for a kind description to fit with reality. 'He was rough but he had a good heart and here he was; I had to show him how to put a nappy on. He'd never seen a disposable nappy in his life. The clips around the grow-wear suit are a bit of a fiddle for anyone and he had these great big gnarly hands! But anyway, eventually he went off and that little boy went back with him to live in Alice Springs. [The dad] said he lost all his friends because he couldn't go to the pub any more; he had a kid now. He used to ring me every few days [asking], "Oh the kid's on the dining room table now, what do I do about that?" "Well, lift him off", I'd say!'

'We'd never been to Central Australia so we decided to go. We went on the train, and as the Ghan rolled in, there he was; there was this dear little boy standing there with this great big bunch of flowers under his arm to welcome us. I felt like the Queen getting off the train. And he was lovely to us. He took us all around and showed us all the sights of Alice Springs. We met up with him each day that we were there, and we went to his home. The little boy slept on a mattress with no sheet on it on the floor. I mean he just lived very differently. He took us to the camel races. It's just red powder all over the ground. It's as dusty as anything. We're walking around there and little Gus is in the stroller and he drops his dummy in the dust. Daddy pulls a tinny out of his back pocket, rinses the dummy off with a splodge of beer and sticks it back in the baby's mouth. I said, "I can't cope". I said, "This is just so different to the way I was bringing up your son". He gave me a nudge and said, "This is the way we do it in the Centre!"'

It has been quite a ride for Carolyn and David Stedman and their family. Like all journeys worth taking, there have been rocky and difficult moments, wrong turns, dead ends, and painful memories. Yet the experience has in many ways defined their lives. 'It's been a lovely thing to do even though there's grief', says Carolyn. 'I don't actually see grief as a negative emotion', she adds, offering me a final piece of wisdom and motherly advice. 'It's an important part of life to be able to grieve.'

In an age of overblown celebrity, hollow media identities, and instant baseless fame, encounters with people of genuine renown are rare. But when you do come across them, you don't forget. Carolyn Stedman's story – one that began and remains within the confines of suburban normality is one of the most remarkable I have heard. In the week that I am writing this, the major newspapers are delivering their lists of celebrities: the 100 Most Influential People of the Year – the 'A-List,' those with 'the X-factor'. Without consulting any of these publications, I know that Carolyn's name won't be there. Instead, there will be the usual suspects: the fashion designers, developers, chefs, celebrities, and writers. Yet it would be hard to imagine anyone having more of an influence for good than her. In delivering relief to human need; in offering comfort and respite to the most defenceless; in putting self-interest aside to create brief moments of light in otherwise very dark places, she is in the true sense, heroic. It is high praise when those closest to you see your life under a microscope over many years and are still impressed. Carolyn's daughter Cate says of her mum, 'I always look at her and think, "I could never be half the person you are"'. I suspect not many of us could.

Ju

'I remember...standing in the middle of the ground and thinking, "Is this as good as it gets?"'

in Langer

Australian Test Cricketer

I didn't know if I should have worn a tie. I was on my way to the Members Pavilion at the Sydney Cricket Ground (SCG) to meet Justin Langer and it occurred to me too late, that the dress code in such a place on game day might dictate higher standards than I was prepared for. I was half expecting not to be allowed in, despite the instructions from my subject to 'ask someone to come and get me'.

' ... Not everybody's necessarily going to like you, and you don't necessarily get on with everyone, but that respect is crucial.'

The official to whom I conveyed this thought, looked at me dubiously, and after an extended silence (ensuring I was suitably uncomfortable), reluctantly led me up the stairs and through the tall glass doors; across the thick red-carpeted grand Members Long Bar that drips with nostalgia and over 130 years of sporting ghosts and memories; beneath chandeliers; past oil paintings of Bradman and O'Reilly and dark-panelled walls and honour boards determined to preserve the memory of heroes past. Eventually we reached the heavy wooden door of the visitor's dressing room. Still looking dubious, he knocked and waited.

On the other side and emerging from the inner sanctum was a track-suited Justin Langer, who greeted me warmly enough to put my reluctant guide at ease. Langer's blue-eyed piercing stare and firm handshake both command and offer respect. The venue for our conversation holds a mystique in Australian sporting history, and is a special place for Langer. It was at the SCG, almost deserted today for an interstate day/night match between NSW and Western Australia, that Langer experienced his final hours of test cricket just over 12 months prior.

Even the most illustrious sporting careers frequently peter out with a whimper rather than a bang, so a glorious finish particularly stands out. Langer chose his moment to depart at the end of a merciless and clinical 5 – 0 defeat of England, completing the 2006/7 Ashes series. He announced his retirement at the beginning of the test, joining Shane Warne and Glenn McGrath in taking a final curtain call. The news added to what was already an emotional occasion. In front of a large crowd on the final day, Langer with his old friend and opening partner Matthew Hayden made a final stand together, marching out to bat chasing only 46 runs to finally put England out of their misery.

'It was a fairy tale end', recalls Langer. 'I was sitting in the change room getting my pads on. Adam Gilchrist came up to me and he was a bit choked up and said, "This is your last innings. I can't believe it, you know". I said, "Yeah, well, no worries mate but get emotional afterwards. I've got to go and bat yet!" And I walked out onto that balcony and my dad was out the front. I shook my dad's hand – he was choked up as well. So I was thinking, "Oh gee!" As we walked out onto the ground, Haydos put his arm around me and said a few words. He was really emotional.'

Amidst the cheers and the tears Langer initially didn't notice the England team forming a guard of honour to greet him in the middle. 'That was the most extraordinary thing', he says. 'That was when it really hit me – that, at the end of my career, I knew I'd earned respect and for me, that's what life's all about. Not everybody's necessarily going to like you, and you don't necessarily get on with everyone, but that respect is crucial. That was a great lesson I learned there. And as it turned out, Mattie Hayden hit a six and a one to win the game and you know, to be out there with him on that big stage, was brilliant.'

Justin Langer and I both spent our childhood playing innumerable backyard test matches in 40-degree heat. The rules at his place may have varied from mine, but he would be able to relate to steaming-in off the long run (pushing off the tank stand); crashing a four through the covers (sneaking a ball between the car and the vegetable garden), being caught in the gully (edging a ball into the lemon tree) and the long walk back to the pavilion (throwing your bat and sulking on your way past the bird aviary and into the house). All the while, the dream of playing for Australia infused our very beings.

But while I have only my South Tamworth Second Grade Premiership cap (sadly still in my possession), Langer made it big time! By the end of the famous retirement day, Langer had played 105 tests, scoring 23 centuries, and 30 fifties at an average of 45.26. No doubt he has a photo album full of countless triumphs around the globe in an era where Australia dominated the cricketing world. Yet, the manner in which his career unfolded makes his story an especially interesting one. After debuting as a gritty middle-order batsman against the fearsome West Indies in 1993, Langer's fortunes fluctuated over the next few years and eventually he lost his place in the team. Many don't ever make it back, but Langer reinvented himself as a fluent and reliable opening batsman. He and Hayden became one of the most formidable partnerships of all time at the top of the order.

His reputation for granite-like toughness reached almost mythical status during his 100th test in Johannesburg. Celebrations of the milestone were short-lived as the only ball Justin played struck him a sickening blow to the head and he spent the next three days concussed and vomiting in bed. At the end of the game with Australia perilously close to defeat, Langer famously dragged himself to the ground and, against strict orders from the doctor who claimed he risked death were he to be hit again, padded up ready to bat. That he wasn't required in the end doesn't diminish the feat. I ask him whether he might have lost perspective at that moment. 'Cricket has been my vehicle for personal development', he explains. 'And in that instance I learned about courage. Everything in my head was telling me, "You can't bat. You can't bat, it's just a game". But my heart was telling me I would hate to let down my teammates.' Langer gained much respect during his career to bounce back from not only the literal hits – of which he absorbed many – but the emotional ones as well.

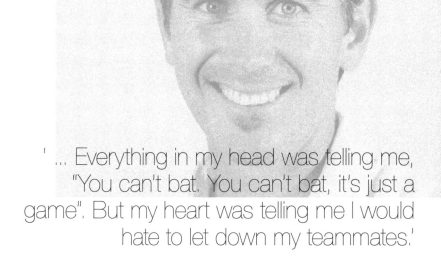

' ... Everything in my head was telling me, "You can't bat. You can't bat, it's just a game". But my heart was telling me I would hate to let down my teammates.'

It is fair to say that Langer is not your average cricketer. An expert in the martial art 'Zen do kai', he also takes great pride in growing roses in his garden. Ferociously fit, Langer is known more for his long gym sessions than sessions in the bar. He is an author of several books – the subjects of which reach beyond the usual bland sporting diary. He is something of an amateur philosopher who is comfortable speaking about spiritual and emotional health, human frailty and telling your dad that you love him. As a father of four girls, he is deeply committed to his family. His decision to retire largely revolved around wanting to be at home more often. He likes to talk about respect, honour, humility and loyalty, which immediately make him something of an anomaly in modern sport.

' ... I remember as clear as day standing in the middle of the ground looking around and thinking, "Is this is as good as it gets?"'

Langer has a perspective on his formidable achievements that make him worth listening to. Thinking back to my own daydreams of sporting fame and glory, I am eager to know whether it all lived up to the dream. The short answer – yes, and no. 'Look, it's been a magnificent journey for me', he says. 'But I look back on my career and I would say 85% of it has just been hard work. I've realised that dreams are really important to keep you focused and motivated, and going in the right direction. But quite often these dreams come at a cost. Playing cricket for Australia is a great example. I received my baggie green cap in Adelaide and it was brilliant, but then I knew I had to go and face the West Indies the next day. If it happens in a dream you can let it run however you want it to run. That's the beautiful thing about dreaming. It's so important for kids to do that but often the dream becomes a bit of a nightmare', he smiles. Those who remember Langer's first outing in Australian colours all speak of the pounding he received from numerous body blows.

Langer admits that he worried too much during his playing days. 'I never allowed myself to get comfortable because I always felt that if you got comfortable you got lazy and I couldn't afford mentally or physically to do that ... I never really let myself relax and enjoy it.'

'Magic moments' frequently come up in conversation with Justin Langer. He describes these with demonstrative actions, and familiar mannerisms as if he is deep in the moment as he relives it. Mostly the sense is one of reward for effort put in; a catch taken at a crucial point in a big game after months of catching practice; a century to win a test after thousands of balls hit against a bowling machine; the satisfaction of shared success with close team mates. 'It must be like when a woman goes through pregnancy for nine months – the pain, the sickness, the agony but then you get this baby!' he says, eyes closed demonstrating the ecstasy of the moment.

But while Langer is happy to relive the many highlights, he also expresses the failure of these triumphs to truly fulfil. A profound moment on one of his biggest days ever serves to illustrate the point. Opening the batting on the morning of the Boxing Day Test against England at the end of 2002, Langer reached his century with a six hit over mid-on. In front of 80 000 fans, including his family, he lived out what would be the script of the perfect day in the world he inhabits, eventually amassing 250 runs and Man of the Match honours.

'It doesn't get better than that', says Langer. 'There's great joy in those moments. It's an intense insane adrenalin rush. But I'll never forget this. I remember as clear as day standing in the middle of the ground looking around and thinking, "Is this is as good as it gets?" and it was great – that was the pinnacle and I do miss that rush. But I still remember it. Maybe it was at tea or in-between overs and I was relaxed on about 140, or 160 or whatever, and I thought, "You know what? This is great, but it only lasts for one second. It's nothing like seeing your baby born, nothing like seeing your baby smile. It's nothing like it, nothing like getting a hug from your dad, you know. We all think it's the greatest thing in the world, but you know what – nah'", he says dismissively.

When the trappings of success failed to produce lasting satisfaction, Langer became increasingly drawn to the question of faith and the place of God in his life. 'I'd been on a tour of Sri Lanka for five or six weeks', he explains. 'I wasn't making any runs. I was away from my newborn baby. It was just a horrible time and I came back and I said to the pastor Andrew Valance, "Mate there's something missing ... I've got everything – I've got a beautiful wife, I've got kids, a big house, beautiful car, nice clothes, plenty of money, but something's missing. I've got a big hole inside and I don't know what it is". He said, "Have you read the Bible lately?" I said, "No, not for a while". The next morning we were flying out to the eastern states. I remember it was a very early flight, maybe a five or six am flight, and he turned up with his wife and three kids to the airport and he handed me this leather-bound Bible. Now you imagine most young blokes get on the plane and read men's magazines and I walked on with a Bible in my hand. I thought there might be a bit of a stigma to it, you know "Bible basher". Anyway I was very thankful that he took the time to give me this Bible and I read it.'

As Langer became more engrossed in what he was reading, he came across a verse that stayed with him. 'It's amazing how life works', he says, 'because I read this Bible verse, Philippians 4 verse 13 – "I can do everything through Christ who strengthens me". I then played in the Second Test in Hobart against Pakistan in 1999. I was under the pump big time for my spot in the team. I had just come from Sri Lanka, I hadn't made any runs and I was under pressure. I went out to bat and I kept saying it like a mantra. I was out in the middle with Adam Gilchrist and I kept saying to myself, "I can achieve anything through God. God give me the strength to achieve anything. God give me the strength to achieve anything". Usually it's "watch the ball, watch the ball, watch the ball". I had to laugh when people commentating on that innings said, "Oh look at his concentration. You know he concentrates so well watching the ball". I wasn't saying, "Watch the ball", I was saying "God give me strength to achieve anything" the whole time. And it turned out to be my greatest ever innings.'

'I said to the pastor Andrew Valance, "Mate there's something missing ... I've got everything – I've got a beautiful wife, I've got kids, a big house, beautiful car, nice clothes, plenty of money, but something's missing, I've got a big hole inside and I don't know what it is".'

'A stepping stone into faith' is the way Langer now describes this time. He had been given some grounding in Bible knowledge as a boy, and is proud to report that he won the Christian Fellowship Award in Grade Seven! It wasn't until later in life as he plied his trade on the cricket grounds of the world that these early seeds came to play a leading role in his life. He has gained much encouragement from his next-door neighbour

Margaret Court – the former World No. 1 female tennis star and winner of 24 Grand Slam Titles. Langer describes her as 'a great Christian woman'. Before a Test in Adelaide Justin was feeling especially nervous and uptight – having difficulty sleeping. He rang Margaret Court in Perth and asked about a Bible verse he was trying to find. 'At the end of a half hour conversation, she said, "It's 2 Timothy 1 verse 7: God does not give us the spirit of fear, but of power and of love and of a sound mind". That sums up life for me', says Langer. 'We have so much depression, so much youth suicide and it's all to do with fear; fear for the future, fear of failure, fear of success, fear of expectation, all these fears. But God doesn't give us a spirit of fear but of love, and of strength and of sound mind. So much of the population has this spirit of fear – you don't want to live like that.'

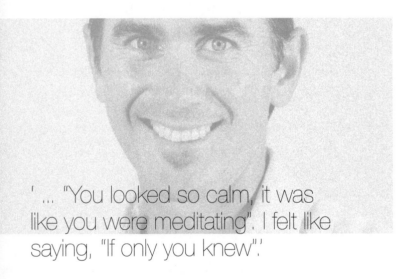

' ... "You looked so calm, it was like you were meditating". I felt like saying, "If only you knew".'

During another Boxing Day Test at the Melbourne Cricket Ground (MCG), Langer stumbled upon a meditative technique that he used in every subsequent game he played. 'Instead of focusing on my breathing or some mantra, I'd been meditating on the symbol of the Cross for a few months. Then when I walked out on to the MCG for the first morning of the Test, I asked for centre, marked the line and began tapping my bat on this brand new wicket and my bat just kept slipping. So I started to scratch the crease so that my bat would go into a rougher surface. I scratched a line across the original mark, and there at my feet was a perfect cross. I did the same thing at the other end and whenever I looked down there was the cross. Two people after that game said, "You looked so calm, it was like you were meditating". I felt like saying, "If only you knew". From that time on Mattie Hayden and I did the same thing. No-one else would know what it was, but we knew and that's all that mattered.'

These days the passionate and intense Justin Langer is more relaxed than he has been for a while. The dominant emotion he says he feels is gratitude. 'I get a lot more joy out of the simple things now', he says. 'I keep a diary and every day I write, "I'm the luckiest person in the world", because I am thankful I've had another great day. I have gratitude for the day. I get great joy working with my roses at home. I love my little baby. My youngest is a two-year-old; all my kids make me so happy. I love them! I'm a serious kind of person but [being] thankful lightens up the whole world for me. I've got a nice house and I've got all that but that's not what I'm most thankful for. We went to England this year – all six of us lived in a very small house, probably a quarter the size of the house in Perth and it was the happiest time of our life. [We were] dancing in the kitchen every day. I was dancing you know. It's hard to be uptight if you're dancing or hard to dance if you're uptight. I'm not sure which one comes first.'

Out of the pressure cooker of international cricket, there is lightness to Langer that is closely connected to his faith. 'I know so many people who are crying out for something', he says. 'They think if they become a Christian it means they've got to give up everything, but I love the story of Jesus and I read it a lot. I see [Christian faith] as having a constant ally. It's not a weight at all, in fact it's the opposite.'

J

'If the Lord can reach me,
he can reach most people.'

Justice
n Gilmour

Federal Court Judge

Whatever image you might be able to conjure in your mind of how a Federal Court Judge might look and act and speak, in the case of Justice John Gilmour, you would almost certainly be wrong. I had my own clichéd preconceptions: old, stooped, pale from a life spent mostly indoors reading incomprehensible documents; an exalted and unapproachable being occasionally descending to impart judgments that impact the common person in ways she will never fully comprehend.

But John Gilmour is much more how you might imagine a rock star ageing gracefully. It would be absolutely no surprise if he were to exit the secure car park at the Federal Court on a Harley Davidson, in leather jacket and kick-head boots; or to catch him playing in a blues band at a pub with old mates; or riding the nose of a long-board in a six-foot swell at Margaret River. I don't know if he does any of those things, but in short – he is very un-judge-like.

But John Gilmour is much more how you might imagine a rock star ageing gracefully.

On the day I meet John in his chambers at the Federal Court building in the centre of Perth, it is sweltering: 40 degrees and it's still only November. He's just returned from a trip to Australia's far northwest, where he had delivered judgment in a large marquee in the middle of the Great Sandy Desert – acknowledging Native

Title in an area of land greater in size than Tasmania in favour of the Ngurrara peoples. Perth is positively cool in comparison, he tells me.

His office is prime ministerially huge, and is everything you would expect in the world of such an eminent official. Shelves filled with gold embossed tomes of law line dark panelled walls. A trolley of large ring-binder folders – an impossible forest of facts to be filtered, absorbed and disseminated – the next case to be heard. The atmosphere is dry, august, and sober. A large window offers a panorama over the Swan River and the more frivolous activities of the city. Below are parks now almost emptied of lunchtime office workers. Bike tracks snake around the edge of the river and in the distance colourful sailing boats pick up the famous Fremantle Doctor to propel them to nowhere in particular.

Tall, with rugged good looks, Gilmour simultaneously conveys authority and kindness. He speaks softly in clear, melodic sentences, fixing his listener with piercing eyes that match the intensity of his character. A hint of a Scottish accent remains but, like his weathered face, his adopted country has worn it down. At only 56, he has a colourful tapestry of experience on which to draw, and a corresponding amount of wisdom to impart. A one-time backpacker, in his early 20s he found his way to Western Australia by accident, and never left. At various points in his life, he has been a farm worker, Cadet Pilot Officer in the Royal Air Force where he gained his pilot's license, barrister, QC and now judge.

When Gilmour speaks of his faith he does so in a manner that is unforced – entirely natural. Perhaps this has something to do with the way he came to Christianity. There are those for whom the journey towards belief is a gentle movement of conviction and acceptance of things long considered or imparted by family and community. For others, it's a 'Damascus Road' experience: more along the lines of having your soul ripped out, and your life turned upside down, and you never recover. This is very much John's story.

Born in 1951 into a family of five children in a small village outside Dundee in Scotland, John's childhood was rural, middle class and mostly happy. Life was essentially school, farm work and sport. And church. 'My father was an elder in the local Church of Scotland and we would go to church every Sunday', says John. 'I can remember my most consistent thoughts about church were that it was really really boring, and secondly I thought that most of the people who went there were hypocrites. And that was based on hard evidence because, unlike our parents, my siblings and I used to spend a lot of time with the local people in the village. We knew what they were like during the week!' he explains. Given the option of staying home on Sundays from the age of 12, John was happy to let that part of his life sink into a distant, vaguely unpleasant past.

By the time he was studying law at university, John was revelling in the self-satisfaction that comes to those who succeed in most things they attempt. His earlier disinterest in Christianity hardened into something more cynical. 'I don't remember at that time having anything other than disdain for most of the Christians I knew', he recalls. 'I mean I was a rugby-playing, drinking bloke probably a bit on the wild side I suspect. Life was pretty good really, and I did all the kinds of things that young university students get up to', he says.

After a couple of years as an apprentice solicitor, Gilmour hit the road of travel and self-discovery. Intending to work his way from Pakistan, across India, South-East Asia, New Zealand, and Canada, before taking up a promised partnership in an Edinburgh law firm, John's progress was halted in Pakistan. In a truly 'Sliding Doors' moment, skirmishes over Kashmir between the Pakistani and Indian armies meant John had to make his next move by air rather than land. Left with a choice of landing in either Bangkok or Perth with only 20 dollars, the decision seemed easy, and so it was that he found himself heading for a family friend's farm at Katanning in the southwest of Western Australia. By the time he got there, 20 dollars became 20 cents, and in a symbolic gesture of rugged individualism and new beginnings, John threw his last coin into a roadside paddock. He began life in Australia with nothing. In every sense he is a self-made man.

Immediately he fell in love – not with a person, that would come later – but with a country. 'I distinctly remember thinking that I really should have been born here', he explains. 'I'm not glorifying it; every nation's got its faults, but I really identified with the Australian way of life. But for that skirmishing between India and Pakistan I wouldn't have come here.' After working on a number of farms, John eventually moved to Perth to resume his legal career.

John threw his last coin into a roadside paddock. He began life in Australia with nothing. In every sense he is a self-made man.

During those years, apart from a few moments of existential struggle, questions of meaning and purpose rarely crossed his mind. 'I remember when I was first out here in Australia particularly down in the country where I was on the farm, the stars were so utterly magnificent and brilliant. I'd look up and I'd think, "I wonder how they got there?" But it was relatively superficial. I never actually strayed beyond that to thinking, "There must be a creator".'

> 'We were playing golf and tennis and going to the pub with this sort of surface happiness but in reality I was deeply unhappy.'

As the Puritan theologian Richard Baxter once said, 'God breaks not all men's hearts the same', and it was only a personal crisis that would crack what, by this time, was John's thick protective armour against anything spiritual. He had fallen in love with Marcia Weller, and while travelling together in Scotland, he proposed. They were married in Edinburgh and then returned to Perth to live. 'We were in a fairly passionate relationship', explains John. 'It was both wonderful and dreadful at the same time. I was around 26. Not so long into our marriage, for reasons that I now understand but didn't then, things started to go wrong. Nothing had actually prepared me for real life. Nothing and no-one had prepared me for what it meant to be married, and my life was filled really with a series of false expectations about what life would be, and what marriage would be, and I was in so many ways immature and frankly ignorant of what was required to live in a right way.'

'Because we were a generation that was at least superficially suggesting that men and women were equal, I thought therefore that if I felt a particular way about something, then so would a woman. I mean how wrong is that? How destined to failure is that?' And fail it did, as the marriage lurched into tumultuous waters. John describes this period of his life as 'very, very distressing'. 'I desperately wanted [the marriage] to work', he says. 'Here was a major venture in my life where I was clearly not successful. The thing that was most important, I was failing in and failing badly. By this time I was a young lawyer in Perth and I was doing very well professionally, but that in a way was point and counter-point. My professional success only underscored the depth of my failure in my marriage and my family life.' The children were beginning to suffer in what was fast becoming a poisonous atmosphere. After a series of attempts to rescue the sinking ship, John finally left. 'I had a great sense of despair', he says of those days.

John moved into a house with a long-time friend whose marriage had also collapsed. 'We were trying to pretend we were fine but we weren't. We were playing golf and tennis and going to the pub with this sort of surface happiness but in reality I was deeply unhappy.' As if things weren't bad enough, during this period John's flat mate became a Christian! 'He was always going on about Jesus and I used to give him heaps. I mean I was fairly hard bitten by then and quite a cynical person probably and certainly immensely antagonistic towards Christianity. But my mate Roger, who is quite a gentle soul, kept on telling me about how his life had changed. It was quite brave of him when I think about it because I wasn't gentle at all. I was the very opposite; I'm sure I was arrogant and difficult and confrontational. Actually, although I fought him on the surface, I could see there was something different about him.'

'Marcia and I had been separated by this time for a number of months and I hadn't seen her at all. [Roger and I] had been to the pub and we were having a beer at home. He was back on his hobbyhorse and I really was getting sick of it. I said to him, "Look Roger, I'll make a deal with you, because I'm getting sick of you going on about Jesus all the time. I will come to the church that you go to and I'll listen to this pastor or whatever it is you call this bloke. Nothing will happen. I will then leave the church and you'll never talk about Jesus again. So that's the deal".' Probably sensing he had little choice in the details of the arrangement, Roger agreed.

So the next morning John hauled himself out of bed to attend a small church in the neighbouring suburb of Subiaco. His mission was to make good on his promise, and to finally get some peace from his persistent, pestering friend. Walking through the front door, the first thing he noticed was that Marcia was sitting among the gathered congregation. Looking back on this moment, he can only think that it was miraculous. Like John, Marcia was no churchgoer. 'The even greater miracle', says John, 'was that I went and sat beside her, because our relationship was not the best. This was early in 1982. On her part, she had been at a party the night before and she was travelling along Bagot Road in Subiaco, and she saw the cross outside the church, which used to be lit up at night with neon lights; she saw the cross and she felt a real desire to stop. She stopped the car outside the church and got out, went over to the cross; she saw the times for the service and she decided she was going to go to church the next day. She actually missed the service that she intended to go to and came to the one that I went to.'

'And I recall this minister, he had no vestments; I was used to ministers wearing a gown. He had a brown blazer on with cream slacks and cream shoes and a striped tie. I remember thinking, "Who is this guy?" Anyway I listened; he gave a message about a guy called Jonah who was called by God to do something and he turned his back on God. A litany of disasters followed him and those whose lives he touched, and I can only say that it was a climactic occasion. It was like my life passed in front of me, and with the same absolute confidence that I had had coming into that church and for all my life that there was no God, when that guy finished preaching the message I knew two things: one, I knew there was a God and two; I knew that he loved me. I can't explain that.'

So began a radically altered life, as John came to embrace the Christian faith he had mostly ignored or derided. The first step was to have another go at his marriage. 'I went back to Marcia and said, "Let's try again". We did that and it wasn't as if there was an instant change in our relationship that cured difficulties. But there was an instant change that enabled me to overcome things that I had not been able to overcome before. I had an inner strength that I had not known before. So we began that reasonably long journey of overcoming all the hurt, all the pain of a fragmented relationship. Because things that get broken like that don't just get fixed in five minutes.'

'For me it's the difference between dark and light. I know what the grace of God means. And it hasn't left me.'

Six months later, Marcia became a Christian, primarily because of the changes she could see in John's life. 'That was 25 years ago and we have together grown in our faith and never, ever thought of giving it up', says John. 'For me it's the difference between dark and light. I know what the grace of God means. And it hasn't left me. It's not some distant memory. As we sit here I can remember that day that I walked into the church.'

As is the case with many people who experience such a dramatic conversion, John has in the years since, been a very public and resolute believer. While working as a barrister, he was a pastor of a church that met in his home for seven years. A love of Scripture marked his faith from the early years in that small church. 'I would read the Bible and it would always make me weep; so it was a very cleansing and healing process that occurred then. I mean I just loved going to church and I still do. I love to hear the word of God preached, because I believe absolutely that it is the life of Christ in words that God's spirit takes to change people, challenge them and convict them', suggests John. 'For me it was so real; this wasn't just a set of rules to live by, this was the reality of the risen Christ.'

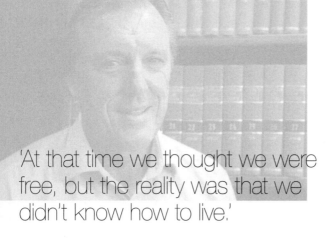

'At that time we thought we were free, but the reality was that we didn't know how to live.'

John firmly believes that God can and does intervene in people's lives in amazing ways, but not always in a manner they might wish for or expect. 'I think God wants to be keenly involved in our lives. There are times when he allows us to go through very difficult things, painful things that will produce character and perseverance and at the time it seems as though he's silent. I don't believe he's not listening, I don't believe he's not interested and I don't believe he's not watching our every move. There's a verse in Romans, Chapter 5, which talks about hope. It says, "…and we give thanks for this hope". It starts with hope but then it says, "We rejoice in this hope even as we rejoice in our suffering, because suffering leads to perseverance and perseverance leads to character; and character, hope. And hope does not disappoint us." So you've got this book-ending of hope, but in-between can be very difficult things.'

John has had some honest wrestling with God over the years especially in moments of pressure and hardship. 'There is a greater reality when you're going through times of testing, and faith has to become a personal possession. I mean faith where you trust God in a dark valley; where you trust God when you don't know what's going to happen; when you trust him when there is no safety net.'

Unlike the 'Sunday Christians' of his childhood, John's faith came to inform every element of his life. Ultimately his approach to family was in no small part affected by his life in the early days of his marriage when things were coming off the rails. 'My views were informed by the half-truths or lies of growing up as a baby boomer in the 60s and early 70s', suggests John. 'We were the first generation who really began to explore and experiment in ways that were foreign to our parents, and utterly foreign to our grandparents. People of our generation were all caught up in that so-called "liberating" atmosphere which actually was thoroughly destructive of what was, I now believe, foundationally important for family life and living. At that time we thought we were free, but the reality was that we didn't know how to live.'

That John was able to build a productive family life was, he says, in large part due to the teaching he received from the Bible and in his church. It saved his marriage, and when it came to raising children, led him to make choices that were counter-cultural in the world of lawyers and barristers. 'I decided I was not going to work on the weekend if I could help it. That was 23 years ago, and I pretty much kept to it. Obviously when there was a big trial I wasn't always able to do it, but 95% of my working life I haven't worked on weekends. ... I made that commitment because that is something I think a father and husband should do and I think [God] honoured that.'

The priority Gilmour placed on family led to some uncomfortable professional moments. More than once he had to resist powerful and influential clients, in order to be present for family gatherings. Mostly, he says, his stand has been respected. No doubt it helped that Gilmour was a highly respected barrister, but his point is well made. 'I don't mean to be self-righteous about this', he explains, 'but I'm just not going to miss out on seeing my family because of work. That's what's wrong with so many families and father/son, father/daughter relationships today. The children know that they're not as important as their dad's meetings with King Kong corporation'.

For such a strong believer, John remains philosophical about those who remain closed or even antagonistic towards the spiritual side of life. 'There are some who are very good at avoiding those sorts of discussions', he says. 'That's frustrating ... but they may be sceptical for good reason because of their experiences, like I was. I don't think my experience of Christianity [when growing up] should have led anyone to anything other than scepticism. It wasn't real. It wasn't the genuine article.'

John Gilmour appears every bit the 'genuine article'. He is very quick to highlight his imperfections and failings, yet spending time with him is to be struck by the power of the Christian story to transform a life. 'When I recall where I was before I became a Christian', says John, 'I'm sure there are many worse cases, but I think if the Lord can reach me, he can reach most people'.

Jo

'Good can come of the most drastic situations.'

ce Harmer

Salvation Army Officer
Court and Prison Chaplain

In C.S. Lewis's speculations of life beyond the grave in his book, *The Great Divorce*, the narrator's ghost is given an introductory tour of heaven by one of the more experienced residents. At one point both the guide and his wide-eyed partner become aware of a great fuss at the imminent arrival of someone of obvious celebrity status. A huge procession of singing and dancing and scattering of flowers approaches – all in honour of one woman being paraded through the streets.

The narrator asks his companion, 'Is this someone who was of great importance on earth – perhaps a famous writer, leader or queen?'

'Who was this relentlessly cheerful, uniformed grandmother enduring day after day of the most gruelling, stomach-churning evidence?'

'It is someone you'll not have heard of', comes the reply.

'She seems to be ... well, a person of particular importance?' says the ghost.

'Aye, she is one of the great ones. Her name on earth was Sarah Smith and she lived at Golders Green', explains the guide. 'Ye have heard that fame in this country and fame on earth are two quite different things', he says.

If C.S. Lewis is touching on something of reality in his contemplation of a heavenly existence, if he understands correctly the likely rewards of a life of service and self-sacrifice, perhaps this is the type of reception that Joyce Harmer can rightly expect when she gets there.

It is a delicious irony, and no doubt a source of some amusement for Major Harmer that late in her career she found herself thrust into the media spotlight. After years of toiling away in relative anonymity as Court and Prison Chaplain at the Downing Centre – the home of local and district courts in the heart of Sydney – two high profile cases briefly catapulted Joyce's name into living rooms and onto breakfast tables across the country. During this brief period her '15 minutes' stretched into months as she made regular appearances on TV current affairs shows, was pursued for radio interviews and discussed in print.

The two cases were equally horrific in nature and both generated a frenzy of media interest. The first was a series of gang rapes in Sydney in 2000. In this instance Joyce provided vital comfort to three of the victims throughout the ordeal of a protracted trial. And then during 2003, Joyce again came to attention as she lent support and spiritual guidance to Kathleen Folbigg, who was eventually convicted of the murder of three and manslaughter of one of her own infant children, making her Australia's worst female serial killer.

Who was this constantly smiling presence, physically and emotionally supporting the hapless women as they dragged themselves into court daily to face the macabre public fascination and collective shame of their plight? Who was this relentlessly cheerful, uniformed grandmother enduring day after day of the most gruelling, stomach-churning evidence? Joyce looked more suited to serving tea and scones at a school fete than being exposed to a barrage of traumatic and violent images, transcripts and witness statements that sickened even hardened detectives and journalists. It wasn't long before people wanted to know who she was. Ultimately, the author Anne Henderson was inspired to write the biography of Major Harmer

– a 300-page treatment of a life spent mostly well away from public notoriety. Indeed it is a story worth telling. The short bursts of publicity that accompanied Joyce's work revealed only an iceberg tip of a life of extraordinary self-sacrifice, personal struggle, compassion and faith.

I meet Joyce at the Downing Centre. It is late afternoon and she has just been to an appeal hearing for Kathleen Folbigg whom she still visits regularly. Joyce is officially retired these days, but is frequently asked to give lunch and dinner talks. As the old Nike ad used to say, 'There is no finish line', a statement no truer than for a life such as Joyce's. She clearly enjoys being back on her old turf – the building mostly deserted today holds many memories for her. Security staff and the odd rushing barrister greet her warmly. Barely 5ft tall, immaculate in full uniform, Joyce beams with optimism, grandmotherly warmth, and empathy. It's not hard to see why judges, cynical lawyers and hardened criminals who have seen it all, would seek her out for counsel and comfort.

Joyce has mixed it with some of the most violent and desperate people in society; many, of course, are at the end of a long line of misadventure when brought before the courts. A man threatening to jump from a window after breaking free of the court officers demanded to see only Joyce. Police, court officials, and professional negotiators had to stand aside while Joyce talked him down from his precarious perch. On another occasion ten officers and copious capsicum spray were required to bring a prisoner under control. He screamed at the judge, 'I wanna speak to Joyce Harmer'. Joyce remembers well the scene that she encountered when she went down to talk to the man. 'He was a mess and he was causing havoc in the holding cells, and he wanted me to ring someone in his family. I said to him, "Mate, I promise you I'll do that for you on one condition ... when the truck comes in for you – don't say yes if you can't – you promise me you'll go quietly. ... Do you think you can promise me that?" and he said, "Yeah I'll promise you that". And so I made the phone call for him but I also waited around the corner to see how he went on the truck. He was like a little lamb. Now that man was hurting. His heart was aching and I felt for him. I don't condone what he did, but God knows the set of circumstances that probably caused a lot of things to happen in his life that you and I haven't had to face.'

'His heart was aching and I felt for him. I don't condone what he did, but God knows the set of circumstances that probably caused a lot of things to happen in his life that you and I haven't had to face'

Growing up in Gympie in Queensland, Joyce's childhood was unremarkable in many respects, but it was clouded by an angry father with a penchant for the strap that left Joyce emotionally scarred. Walking a tightrope of unpredictable verbal, physical and emotional abuse, Joyce had many reasons to feel glad marrying Hilton when she was only 20: to escape the town of her youth and make a new life.

As a teenager Joyce had responded to the Salvation Army equivalent of an altar call, and began a spiritual journey she is still on. Both Joyce and Hilton were deeply committed to the Salvos and their concern for the broken and the lost. They became officers and embarked on a life of rare selflessness, picking up the pieces of destitute lives on the fringes of society. That life took many forms including feeding the homeless; living with and providing shelter and rehabilitation to drug addicts and alcoholics; managing Salvation Army stores to raise money and provide furniture, bedding and other necessities for people down on their luck. It was church work that always looked outwards to practical action. No task was ever too much trouble. The Harmers were transferred frequently and seemingly without thought for their own comfort or sense of home. They always answered the call of their church. Eventually that call took Joyce to the court and the role she is most known for.

'God's given us all these varying abilities to do things and we waste our life unless we pick up where our gift is.'

In Joyce's mind, none of this is worthy of accolade. She was just being obedient to God. 'My gift is caring for people', she says. 'That is where I feel I am so comfortable because I can be me. And God uses our personalities and that's why we're so different. God's given us all these varying abilities to do things and we waste our life unless we pick up where our gift is', she says. Joyce has been known to chase after crying women she has noticed in airports or in shopping centres, to offer assistance. 'I can't help myself', she says. 'Wherever I go I'm looking for people and I just see people. I'm walking down the street and if I see someone wiping a tear from their eye, I have to go and say, "Is there something I can do?" I carry my business card and say, "Look this is who I am", because I'm not always in uniform. My feeling is this: God has given us eyes, ears and a mouth and we have to use them. If you see someone who's in a distressed situation or you hear of someone in your street or anywhere, and you know that they need some particular kind of help, contact someone if you can't do it yourself but don't let it go unattended.'

From the very beginning of their lives together, Joyce and Hilton embraced a brand of Christian faith that was centred on Christ and sought to meet human need. Joyce preached in church for 20 years, but became convinced her gifts lay elsewhere. It was Christianity with its sleeves rolled up, which her father used to say was 'the only sort that matters'. 'I believe that God called me to serve and to do and I can't find a way I can comfortably serve without doing – I have to. I'm compelled to', says Joyce.

When she arrived at the court as Chaplain, Joyce had to construct a job out of a previously non-existent position. 'My work in the court was one of trying to show the compassion of Jesus in doing and hugging. Many times a hug and a handkerchief meant so much to so many people because what does someone do if they're distressed and all they have is a tissue? I pray where the opportunity arises and on many occasions in the ladies' bathroom I've had my arms around women who've sobbed on my shoulder. In fact nine times out of ten there's makeup all over that left shoulder', says Joyce pointing proudly to the uniform that looks virtually new to me.

The list of duties performed at the court by Joyce (with Hilton's assistance) looks exhausting. I feel sorry for whoever was her successor! The Harmers were literally available to people around the clock. Supporting victims and perpetrators of crime, and their families, they met relatives at airports and train stations and arranged accommodation for people from out of town and overseas. They provided counselling for drug and alcohol addiction, gambling habits and troubled marriages.

They cleaned out flats and stored belongings for the incarcerated, and ran errands for those tied up in the court system. They sat in interviews between police and the accused, went to homes to inform relatives of court outcomes, took flowers to graves, conducted weddings, christenings and funerals.

There are some who find it difficult to stomach the concern Joyce has for not only the victims of terrible crimes, but also the perpetrators. She has come under criticism for this but insists her actions are what she is required to do. There isn't anyone that Joyce believes is too far-gone to warrant her attention. 'No, I can't cast them aside', she affirms. 'Because Jesus said that if we confess our sin he's faithful and just and will forgive us, cleanse us and clean our lives up and so you know that's the message I inevitably give people. ... I don't condone crime but I don't condemn the person who did something in a fit of rage, which is a tragedy. I mean so many cases I've been in are like that. I'm not the judge. I pick up pieces of broken humanity in the name of Jesus under the sign of the Cross.'

Joyce's ability to empathise with others, no doubt comes in part from her own very real struggles and her honesty in confronting them. She has had her own demons to contend with. A severe bout of Post Natal Depression (PND) suffered after the birth of her third child – a daughter, Lyndall – brought Joyce into a place of great need. 'I felt like I was in a closed bottle and I couldn't escape', she explains. PND is not widely understood today, but in the 1960s was even less so. Joyce is now just grateful she didn't do anything to harm herself or her baby. For months Hilton took over the parental duties and eventually with medication, time and rest she recovered, but the experience left its mark. I wonder aloud whether that helped her sympathise with Kathleen Folbigg. Joyce says Folbigg never admitted guilt, so it is a moot point.

When pregnant with her fourth child, Joyce's husband Hilton was struck down with Encephalitis and was given 48 hours to live. He survived, but the illness dramatically affected his personality. A caring, kind, thoughtful and loving husband suddenly became depressed, angry, and hot-tempered. 'There were occasions when

I had to keep the children out of his way', remembers Joyce, of a time she says was deeply traumatic. The sad irony of a return to a household dominated by fear and anger was especially poignant. For years Hilton struggled to recover his old self, and by his own admission had become self-pitying and extremely difficult to live with. Great strain was placed on the marriage. Typically Joyce hung in there and weathered the storm that lasted years. 'She is one hell of a woman and a saint to put up with what I pushed on her in those days', says Hilton.[3]

Perhaps the cruellest blow, however, came when the Harmer's fourth son Athol, got mixed up in drugs. Given their years of caring for addicts this must have cut deeply.

Perhaps the cruellest blow, however, came when the Harmer's fourth son Athol, got mixed up in drugs. Given their years of caring for addicts this must have cut deeply. Athol came to his mum at the court and admitted to an addiction lasting around seven years and that his marriage was in tatters. Joyce and Hilton just did what they always did in a crisis – they 'prayed

3. Quoted in Anne Henderson, *An Angel in the Court*, (Harper Collins Publishers, Australia 2005), page 115

like mad and loved him through it', says Joyce, and eventually 'God turned their whole life around'. Today Athol and his wife are Salvation Army officers, working with underprivileged youth in Sydney's West.

'The tragedies of life equip you to see right into the hearts, and the minds, lives and needs of those people who are passing through a similar experience.'

There is a raw honesty in the way Joyce speaks about herself and her motivation for doing so is all about helping others. 'Never be afraid to share your life story', she counsels. 'Someone might be struggling with the very thing you are tempted to hide. The tragedies of life equip you to see right into the hearts, and the minds, lives and needs of those people who are passing through a similar experience', says Joyce. 'The things you've been through equip you for the future; you can use them as a tool or they can drag you down. You've got a choice.'

This notion of choice is a strong theme in conversation with Joyce, and this is seen powerfully in her approach to forgiveness. Over time, she says she was able to forgive her father, and from that decision she attained a freedom she hadn't thought possible. 'Good can come out of the most drastic situations', says Joyce.

'While my father and I didn't get along together and there was quite harsh discipline to me particularly, I've been able to forgive him. And forgiveness is so important and one never knows what release of spirit is until we release resentment or we forgive someone. I tell people, "Only you can do that".' For Joyce there is an undeniable spiritual element to this. 'I couldn't have forgiven my father for – physical abuse it would be called today – without the Holy Spirit within me, without a spiritual concept of the whole thing of forgiveness. I thank Jesus for that, because without him I wouldn't even be here', says Joyce.

When I ask Joyce about the things that give her the most joy she talks about family, her grandkids and her husband. She briefly mentions food and chocolate but soon her thoughts turn to work and the stories of redemption in which she has had a ringside seat. Visits to former prisoners, who have turned their lives around, rate highly on her scale of best moments. 'We have some beautiful stories. There's a man who slashed his wrists and stomach in front of his children. The marriage broke down and we used to supervise the access visits because he couldn't be with the children on his own. We've grown to love them, they give us Christmas presents and we go out to see them. They're all united together and he now goes to Mass every Sunday. When I first met him in the cells he was a pitiful sight; he hated himself for what he'd done. But you know God and his goodness has brought good out of that terrible situation and now they just love each other to bits.'

Despite all that Joyce has witnessed and experienced personally, she brims with an optimism that is disarming. She has a remarkable trust in the redemptive potential of even the most spectacular examples of human wreckage. 'I just look, not for what the person is, but what they can be', she says. 'I know that God can bring good out of any situation. I say to people, "You don't get out of a train in a tunnel and you don't get out of your set of circumstances by doing anything stupid while you're in the tunnel of doubt or exasperation. You stay there until things lighten up".'

'I believe when we pray to God he answers', says Joyce. 'I believe he answers one of three ways: "Yes", "No" and sometimes simply, "Wait". And that's the hardest of all to do. But he always answers. It's not always how we want it because he knows us better than we know ourselves. So it's yes, no or wait.'

An unfailing belief in the benefit of making right choices, gives Joyce hope even for those who are seemingly lost to alcohol and drug addiction. 'It's as far away and as close as a prayer', says Joyce. 'They've just got to get to a point where they crave a better way of life like they crave their alcohol and drugs.' Of course for Joyce that better life revolves around Jesus and the faith she first accepted as a teenager. This is the life that she says has given her more than she could have imagined.

She describes that life as 'beautiful', 'rewarding' and 'rich', but not in the way many would regard as carrying mass appeal in the supermarket of faith options. Indeed Joyce's promotion of her faith is quiet, understated yet resolute. It's one-on-one. It comes with a hug and a hanky and a hot meal. It is delivered through practical help and sometimes without a word. It comes by way of a compelling personal story of survival and hope shared with openness and honesty. 'I don't believe in pressurising people', explains Joyce. 'I can only tell them what happened to me, and I like to say, "This worked for me mate, and if you try it, it just might work for you".'

Joyce carries a simple card with a Salvation Army crest and her phone number wherever she goes, handing it out to anyone who looks troubled, distressed, angry, lost or in need of care. She fears neither the encounter, nor the time and effort it might cost to be of any real help. Who knows how many of those cards have been handed out over the years? I have one and I'm hanging on to it – just in case.

'I know my God is
faithful because I have
experienced that.'
Rachel Watt

Cameron&
chel Watt

Survivors of prison life

Paul Kelly's 1997 hit *How to make gravy* is a song of longing and regret. Joe, a father and family man phones his brother from prison. Christmas is approaching. Imagining his large family opening presents and roasting the turkey, he reminisces about his past role in the annual rituals. Joe says, 'Who's gonna make the gravy now? I bet it won't taste the same'. The song conveys piercing sadness but also nostalgia for the things we so often take for granted. 'Won't you kiss my kids on Christmas day, please don't let 'em cry for me', begs Joe. And in sending his love to the tribe, Kelly's mournful tone delivers the line, 'Tell 'em all I'm sorry. I screwed up this time.' If Cameron Watt knows the song, he can no doubt relate to it more than most.

... once caught out, the enormity of what he and his family faced pressed upon them with unceasing, suffocating misery.

In 2004, Watt was sentenced to four years' imprisonment with a non-parole period of two years and six months. He was 29 years old. He'd never even had a speeding fine. A country boy from the NSW north coast, he had come to the city for university, and stayed. He married Rachel in 1997 when she was only 18 and he 24. They were church-going people. He had a degree and was working for a Christian finance company. There was nothing in Cameron's past that would have indicated the path he was eventually to take. Unlike the many for whom prison is no real surprise, there were no brushes with the law, no acts of spontaneous violence, no stolen cars or reckless behaviour.

Cameron's crime was starchy white-collar. His charges: 11 counts of dishonestly using his position as an employee of a company, with the intention of directly or indirectly gaining advantage for himself. You can read about the case in a stark, officious entry on *The Australian Securities and Investments Commission* website. It tells only a tiny part of the story.

Becoming Assistant General Manager of Baptist Investments and Finance Ltd, at what he now sees was too young an age, Cameron invested company money in a risky off-shore scheme. At the same time he was syphoning significant amounts of money from company funds for his personal benefit. This worked well for a while. No-one was there to look over his shoulder. He figured the returns on the investment would be more than enough to pay the money back without anyone noticing.

Then the planes hit the towers in the September attacks on New York City. The investment collapsed and Cameron's gamble had failed. He had cost his employer millions.

He was called to an extraordinary board meeting on a Sunday. 'I knew that it was very serious', says Cameron. 'I was in there for about three hours or so ... after which Rachel and I just sat in the car and balled our eyes out', he recalls. Cameron's misdemeanours had been discovered and once caught out, the enormity of what he and his family faced pressed upon them with unceasing, suffocating misery. For Rachel this was both a heart-racing, breathtaking shock, and slow dawning terror for what the future might hold. She had been oblivious to the financial infidelities of her husband. For Cameron, the shame and embarrassment meant that even at this point he only gradually revealed details of the case to her.

The legal treadmill stretched on for years until in 2003 the matter finally went before the courts. For three years they had waited for the trial, the final result constantly hanging over the couple's heads. 'It taints everything', says Rachel. 'The birth of children, birthdays, anniversaries, everything is tainted by the knowledge of what may happen.'

Cameron says that even as he went into the trial, he still wasn't being honest with himself regarding the extent of his personal culpability. 'I thought of myself as a victim. I was trying to blame everyone else.' At a critical moment in the proceedings, Cameron had what Rachel calls his 'moment of character'. It was a flash of clear thinking, a point of self-realisation that devastated his chances of success, but arguably, made him as a person. Cameron was in the witness stand. The case was far from secure but he was, as he puts it, 'still in with a fight'.

'I was in the middle of my barrister taking me through my time in the stand', says Cameron. 'One of his questions went along the lines of, "So, Mr Watt, do you believe what you did was dishonest?" I stopped to think about it just for a couple of seconds. It felt like a longer time, but it was probably only a few seconds and it was at that point – and this was years after the event where I had been continually saying not only to other people, but even to Rachel, "Oh, you know, I don't think what I did was that bad …" – that I actually said, "Yes it was dishonest!" My poor barrister nearly fell on the ground, and he was shuffling papers and saying, "Ah, Mr Watt, did you really mean to say dishonest or did you mean …". At that point the judge stopped proceedings; he made the jury go out of the room and then he said to my barrister, "Look you need to talk to your client," and "Do you understand what you have actually just said, Mr Watt?" But truthfully it was a real relief for me to finally just be able to say, "I did the wrong thing. I now know I shouldn't have done it".'

Cameron's mother, who was in the court that day says it was the proudest she has ever been of him. This came from a woman who was as shocked as anyone to see her son in the position he had managed to get himself into. Cameron explains that 'whilst it was detrimental to our case, it was monumental to my growth as a Christian. It was at that point of me being stripped back of all defences ... that God was saying to me, "Cameron you can continue to justify yourself or I can justify you completely". So it was a real turning point', he says.

When I meet Cameron and Rachel in their home in Sydney's leafy northwest they are less than a year beyond the ordeal of two and a half years of prison time. Their journey is a tale of survival, and reconstruction. There is nothing in their demeanour that would immediately betray the emotional scars you might expect to see in two people who have gone through such a drawn-out crisis. Perhaps just a wisdom and understanding beyond their years, a legacy of the experience.

'But truthfully it was a real relief for me to finally just be able to say, "I did the wrong thing, I now know I shouldn't have done it".'

That experience essentially saw Cameron swapping a business suit for a baggy green uniform, and Dunlop Volley shoes so outdated they are now retro fashion items. He was taken from his 24-year-old wife and three kids – the youngest only four months old – to join other inmates for what, at the beginning, must have seemed like an eternity. Just like the other fallen corporate miscreants who actually get caught and spend time behind bars, Cameron was thrust among a group of people from worlds utterly foreign to him.

'Basically my faith in God was one of the only things that kept us going, because it would have been easier to walk away ... '

Cameron certainly did the wrong thing, and he paid for it. The first Christmas day spent in prison, when Rachel and the kids had to come in for an hour and then go away, was especially tough. 'I was so totally distraught ... it was just a horrific feeling', remembers Cameron. 'Thankfully I had a great cell-mate who knew how upset I was going to be, and he walked out and let me be in the room for an hour.'

Prisoners say the first six months of any sentence is the hardest. Visits from Rachel and the family were every Saturday from 8.30am to 3pm, and most Sunday afternoons. 'Although it was wonderful to have that time', says Rachel, 'it was also stressful. It's a visitors' room; there are guards walking around. You are supposed to sit at a table. We had children toilet training. The only food available was from vending machines', she says.

But it was in jail, as he began to come to grips with all that had happened that Cameron says he first started to take his Christian faith seriously. 'I think for so long, while I had been a Christian, my life had been just so dominated by every thought and whim about *me*. Yet when I was brought to that point of brokenness, having lost my whole reputation, God put me in a place where I couldn't rely on myself any more', he says. 'It was really a place where God had to bring me to change the way I saw everything. I would never have committed another crime if I had not gone to jail, but I don't think I would have changed to the extent that I did by just being scared of going to jail. God needed to bring me to that low point where all I could do was look up at him.'

This sparked something of a personal revival of faith for Cameron. He found himself constantly talking with other inmates about spiritual matters, and he became heavily involved in the prison Christian fellowship. On a night when Cameron had addressed an open meeting of the Christian group attended by a large number of inmates, he was waiting in line to phone Rachel, when three members of a powerful bikie gang approached him. He immediately assumed they had taken exception to his talk and were going to bash him. 'I thought, "I'm glad I'm near the guard station because the guards will see me get hit fairly quickly. So I won't actually be killed, I'll just be hurt,' says Cameron. In fact, they came with an offer of protection. Apparently approving of the talk Cameron had delivered, the leader said, 'If anything happens in the jail, you come and tell us and then just forget about it, and we'll take care of it'. While he didn't take them up on the offer, Cameron says he became mates with these men, regularly speaking together and sharing dinners. Presumably exercise yard time took on a more relaxed feel after this!

An extraordinary aspect of this couple's story is that their marriage today is stronger than ever. Rachel admits there were tremendous strains placed on the relationship as they went through the ordeal. 'My commitment was 100% to those marriage vows. Of course I didn't anticipate that that's where it would lead, but I was committed to him. Basically my faith in God was one of the only things that kept us going, because it would have been easier to walk away and it would have been easier to say, "This is not what I signed up for, I'm sorry but you're on your own".'

That she not only stayed, but was able to hang in there and make a solid marriage out of the mess, is a testament to her character and to her trust in a power beyond herself. 'Our faith was in a God who doesn't change even though our circumstances changed so dramatically', explains Rachel.

There is something grounded and authentic about the way both Rachel and Cameron speak about their experience. They don't whitewash it or trot out answers to please the listener. 'There were dark moments', says Rachel. 'It was a real journey. I was never sheltered from the harshness of it. I was never miraculously not tired ... but I never felt abandoned by God. I was always sure of God's love even in the midst of it.'

Rachel admits that in the early years of the ordeal, and as the trial commenced, she assumed God would rescue her family from their greatest fear – prison time. 'It was a really long process of recognising that I really had a wrong concept of who God was. ... I had seen God as more of a fairy godmother who could fix things and wave a magic wand and make things better. But the reality is that we make mistakes and we have to face the consequences of those choices, and to be honest I think the real growth came for me in trusting him through the consequences. So instead of a miraculous verdict [of not guilty] which would have been wonderful, in a lot of ways we have learnt so much more going through it rather than being delivered from it.'

This notion of God's power to redeem a bad situation is a strong theme of conversation with these two. 'I am more optimistic about what God can do and I can look at an event in life, however good, bad or in between it is, and see how God can work in and through it', says Cameron. 'At the start of my time in jail, all these well-meaning Christians told me, you know "all things work together for the good for those who love God and are called according to his purposes", and I thought, "Well thanks very much, and how about you come and sit in jail and have your family separated from you and see how you feel then". But I got to the point of being able to thank God for sending me to jail, and that's such a weird thing to actually say to people, but I got to see how amazingly God can transform and move a person's life.'

'I had seen God as more of a fairy godmother who could fix things and wave a magic wand and make things better. But the reality is that we make mistakes and we have to face the consequences of those choices ... '

A sense of assurance is what Rachel clings to. 'We know there are other things that will go wrong. We know there are going to be times in life when we feel that things are stripped away again, but we are assured that we know where our hope is, where our future is and that's not going to be shaken', she says. 'God is walking before us, and beside us, and with us and in that respect I'm not scared of the future like I could be.'

One of the more lasting compensations to emerge from the ashes of this chapter of the Watt family's life, is what they feel is a greater capacity to empathise with others. Contact with people from 'the other side of the tracks', with stories much more painful than their own, has helped them appreciate what they have, and offer support to others. 'I think our lives were just so sheltered', says Rachel, who continues her involvement in the Christian support group for partners of inmates. 'You can't help but be involved in seeing the pain of what they are going through', says Cameron, who is acutely aware of the life circumstances that push some people towards prison from the earliest of ages.

'Our priorities were in financial security or having a home. ... Now we know where our security comes from.'

Christians are at times perceived as favouring religiosity over relationships; ritual and form ahead of substance. Sometimes this criticism is fair. But there is no such problem for the Christians in prison, says Cameron. 'I think you find that while Christians in jail may not be as refined as middle-class Australia likes Christians to be, they just have a truthfulness in their faith in God. It blew me away in one of the first chapel services that I went to, that this guy was praying and he was swearing. I sat there thinking, "Oh man this is so bad. I should stop this guy. I feel like I need to stop him". Yet I looked and I saw how fervently he was praying. His prayers were so heart-felt with these swear words in them. It made me realise, God's a God who can handle swearing. He doesn't care about swearing, he cares about where your heart is.'

Such raw honesty has rubbed off on Cameron and Rachel. 'If we can't be real with each other, it's just so fake', says Rachel, explaining how they now try to live in whatever community they are a part of. And acceptance at church has been another, perhaps surprisingly positive aspect of the story. 'When we first started attending I went as a single mum with three children whose husband was in prison', reports Rachel. 'We have felt totally accepted. Our senior minister likes to say, "No matter what you've done, no matter what you've become, there's still a place for you to call home". And we have found that 100%.'

They are both disarmingly open about who they are and what they have been through. I saw Cameron recount his story in a church context, and he in no way tried to gloss over his guilt, or the pain that his family experienced. I wonder about the stigma of a past conviction and having served time, but both Cameron and Rachel feel that so far, people have been kind and accepting. It no doubt helps that both their families were so supportive from the moment things began to unravel. Even Rachel's family who, let's face it, could be forgiven for wanting to disown Cameron, were quickly able to put aside their feelings of betrayal and get behind the beleaguered couple. Rachel's grandmother made a regular Sunday morning visit to the jail, to make sure Cameron was not without a visitor during that part of the day.

These days Cameron is studying theology. Rachel has given birth to the couple's fourth child. Now aged 33, Cameron is older and wiser – the experience of prison has, no doubt, given him the perspective of a much older man. Still, he jokes about time standing still while behind bars. 'I feel I should be 30. It's only fair. I missed out on the birthdays!'

But life isn't the same. 'I think God has brought us through a process of change that I don't think we could undo, or go back to who we were before', says Rachel. 'Our priorities were in financial security or having a home. ... Now we know where our security comes from. A home, reputation, relationship, everything can be stripped away, but [our] relationship with God can't be, so that's where our priority is now.'

Andr

'You don't realise how bright things are until you've seen how dark the night can be.'

Scipione

NSW Police Commissioner

Andrew Scipione is a supreme optimist. He is the only person over 45 I have ever heard sing the praises of Generation Y. Admittedly his own children are in that bracket, but nonetheless, he sounds entirely sincere when he speaks glowingly of a section of the population typically described as disorganised, uncommitted, street-wise, cynical and disrespectful. Not Scipione. He sounds positively fond of them and claims their ability to cope with change and their willingness to embrace multiple careers means they are well placed to lead the way toward a bright future.

And he must have a reasonably buoyant view of the world to agree to take on the job of New South Wales' top policeman just days before the largest security operation in the nation's history: at the APEC conference in September 2007, Sydney played host to the Head of State of every major nation on the planet. Scipione had a lot to lose on that occasion, and apart from a motorcade of comedians penetrating the restricted zone where they were only a jittery sniper's finger away from instant death, he came through with his reputation intact.

And it is quite a reputation that 'A.P. Scipione APM MM' has built in his 28 years of service. Having joined the NSW Police Force in 1980, Scipione combined conscientious, intelligent policing with strong academic qualifications to progress through the ranks to his current lofty position. His enormous corner office in the CBD towers over Sydney's Hyde Park, with views past St Mary's Cathedral to the harbour in the distance. Seated on a large green studded-leather lounge sipping tea from official police china, he is a world away from the gritty environment of Bankstown station where he was once a young detective, or even Kings Cross where he worked in the 1980s – visible today through the large plate glass. Yet Scipione hasn't lost touch with those on the ground and you get the feeling he spends very little time enjoying the view. I see him at 8.30am, and my impression is he is well into his day.

Scipione was a popular choice to take over the job of Commissioner. In his many and varied roles he has earned a reputation for professionalism, teamwork and astute judgement.

He has been a senior advisor on counter-terrorism, worked with the National Crime Authority and was in charge of Internal Affairs when he was Assistant Commissioner. He has gained experience and training from around the world in combatting organised crime and is a graduate of the FBI's National Executive Institute in Washington. Well known for integrity, unfailing honesty and competence, he was well credentialed to take over the administration of one of the world's largest police forces. 'My job is pretty simple. It's to provide strategic leadership to 20 000 people', he says with only a trace of irony.

'Well-known for integrity, unfailing honesty and competence, he was well credentialed to take over the administration of the one of the world's largest police forces.'

At 48, Scipione looks strong and fit and he brims with energy. He views the world through eyes that see clear choices of good and bad, right and wrong. While he has witnessed plenty of the less uplifting aspects of human interaction, and had to deal with personal loss, you get the feeling he hasn't spent much time on the psychologist's couch processing any of this. He is not a navel-gazing type. He plays down his achievements, while providing thoughtful measured answers. He is fully present for our conversation despite his phone beeping incessantly. There is work to be done in protecting the state, but he is gracious with his time.

At only 14, Scipione faced the jolting intrusion of death at close range and a disorientating, uncertain future without his dad.

Scipione was born in England but came to Australia as a baby, when his Irish mother and Italian father decided to chance their arm in the Australian version of the new world with all its promise of opportunity and fresh beginnings. The family settled in southwestern Sydney where Scipione says he experienced a carefree childhood of play, adventure and strong community. He loved football, swimming and collecting tadpoles from the creek that ran through the back of his property. His descriptions of cracker night and suburban innocence conjure up the type of nostalgic retro images typically exploited by advertisers when drawing on anything 60s. His memories of childhood are virtually all positive.

Then his father died. At only 14, Scipione faced the jolting intrusion of death at close range and a disorientating, uncertain future without his dad. 'He died at home and I can recall the morning vividly and sitting there thinking "What now?"' recalls Scipione. His much older sister had left home and so it was only he and his mother left to forge a life out of the rubble of loss and the aching loneliness of the migrant family, far from kin and country. This loss, as is so often the case with successful people, became the dominant shaping motif of Scipione's life.

His world, and that of his mother, was in ruins but he was determined that it would not destroy them. Somewhere in the heart of the 14-year-old boy, emerged a steely resolve. 'I went from being a boy to the man of the household overnight', he explains. 'It taught me the importance of being independent, and being strong and being there for others. I think that stayed with me, that notion of strength of character and understanding that through adversity you can develop.' Scipione's mother took on shift work to meet mortgage payments, and he could not afford to be a drain on the household. He left school at 15 to seek an apprenticeship.

Scipione had become a Christian six months prior to his father's death and, if he needed any help to understand that such a decision wouldn't protect him from the vagaries of life, this was surely it. The Scipiones were not religious people, but the young couple that had moved in next door were, and they had a lasting impact on Andrew. He remembers them being especially kind and interested in him as a person. 'I can recall sometimes where I'd just drop in and probably be a nuisance', he says. 'They were a constant in my life and were always good role models.' Over time this couple invited Scipione to the youth group they ran at the local church and he felt an immediate magnetic attraction to what the group embodied. 'It would have to have been the sense of life, vitality and excitement in the people that I was around in those days', he explains. 'These were young people of my age; some were a little older. They had all the same problems but they had a sense of purpose. They weren't aimless but really enjoyed life. They had this depth of understanding that there was more to life than just what we saw around us. And that was attractive.'

There might be many who would interpret a devastating loss such as the one Scipione experienced when he lost his father, as evidence that his newly adopted faith had little security to offer. But his reaction was the opposite. He admits it was a daunting task to suddenly have to act responsibly and look after his mother. 'It taught me to rely on God's promises', he says. 'God's word says, "I can do all things through Christ because he's going to give me the strength to do it." And it was about strength, not ability. It didn't mean I stopped being a typical teenage boy overnight but it meant I could achieve things through reliance on [God] and having a belief in myself because I trusted that God would enable me. It's a lasting legacy that stays with me today. I've taught my children – my boys and my daughter – that they can do it, all that God's got planned, because he's going to be there with them.'

When he reflects on the period of his life when he lost his father, he can see good things emerging out the desolation. 'I am convinced I was looked after. That deepened my relationship and sense of trust and faith knowing that God is there for those who put their trust in him.' He adds, 'When you don't have an earthly father, you're more reliant on [your] Heavenly Father. There are good times and tough times and God's the God of all of them'.

When Andrew Scipione speaks about his faith, it's not pushy or forced, but a simple recognition of what it has brought to his life. He says his approach has been to ask God, 'What have you got in store for me today?' and simply trust that he would always be there for him. 'And that's a wonderful assurance whether you're a young boy, a teenager, a young adult, a father, a brand new father or a middle-aged executive. It's that childlike faith of saying, "I'm going to trust you". When my young sons and my daughter were only toddlers of three, four, five [years old] at the swimming pool, I used to stand in the deep end and say, "Jump into my arms" and they always knew that I'd be there to lift them up and say, "It's okay". And that's the childlike faith that I am sure I carried through into my professional career, into my family life, into my personal experience. I don't know that this life's too complex. We make it complex but I don't know that it really is.' And to those who don't believe or are not convinced, Scipione merely says, 'I can't talk about anyone else, but I can tell you what happened to me'.

'When you don't have an earthly father, you're more reliant on [your] heavenly father. There are good times and tough times and God's the God of all of them'

Any length of time spent in the Police Force will expose you to the shadier aspects of humanity. This is as true at the level of domestic violence, as it is in contact with sophisticated drug cartels. Scipione must have seen his fair share of ugliness, but he manages to hold on to a very positive view of life and of people. '[Firstly] it makes you grateful for what you've got', he says. 'It gives you a really good understanding of how good your life is ... and how balanced and stable it is. You don't realise how bright things are until you've seen how dark the night can be. And you see dark nights. The other thing it showed was you can actually contribute and make an enormous difference to an individual, to a community, to a nation', he adds. Scipione is quick to highlight the positive aspects of each community he has worked in, and the number of admirable people in them.

'If you treat people well, you generally get a much better outcome, be they a murderer, a drug importer or someone who has committed a traffic infringement.'

An Old Testament verse from the Prophet Micah calling Israel 'to act justly, to love mercy, and to walk humbly with your God' provides a framework in which Scipione sees himself operating. 'What I bring to this particular position, I believe, is a sense of honesty and integrity; not perfectionism because no-one's perfect and certainly I've made my mistakes and will continue to. But I try to be gracious because I've been forgiven much. So, there are three basic tenets here for me and that's to, first and foremost, act justly in everything I do. [Secondly] to show grace ... this notion of being merciful. [Thirdly] to remain humble, because humility is so important when it comes to people who can exercise power, to understand that you don't have a God- given right to judge people. You're here to do a job in the interests of the community.'

The Commissioner sees no tension between justice and mercy, and is no soft touch. He certainly secured many convictions as a detective. 'You can administer justice by treating somebody well', he explains. 'That doesn't mean [you've] got to let them go.' It does mean not acting unjustly in order to secure a conviction; along with ensuring even the criminals have their rights protected. 'If you treat people well, you generally get a much better outcome, be they a murderer, a drug importer or someone who has committed a traffic infringement.'

Scipione talks a lot about servant leadership – by which he means the type of leadership that is interested in listening, building community, personal development of staff, models of high ethical standards, and empathy. This sits well with his Christian convictions, and he says, it happens to work. 'The top 500 organisations in the U.S. consistently model their business around servant leadership', he says. 'It's not just the model for the Christian. It's a successful business model that many non-Christian corporations have taken on and they've just excelled.'

One part of Scipione's mission centres on fighting corruption, not only from outside but within the force, and it is in this area he is clearly unbending. It is as simple as clear choices made with their consequences in mind. 'Corruption is like rust in a car. Often you don't know it's there until it's too late and it's broken through the paintwork', he says. He emphasises that the vast majority of police officers in his force are hardworking and honest, but stresses that young officers have to make good choices early in their career if they are to stay clean. Any pressure to waver from the straight and narrow path must be taken head on. 'You've got to send those messages very early', he says. In Scipione's case, his Christian faith gave him the confidence to be strong in his convictions, because his identity came from his sense of acceptance by God, rather than others. 'You've got to have the moral courage and the strength to be able to say, "Don't even try and think about me in those terms because that's not the way I conduct myself, it's not going to happen". And that message doesn't need to be given twice, but you've got to make it very early and it's got to be very clear.'

In a career in which he has capitalised on each opportunity presented to him, he has few regrets, apart from those to do with family. 'I guess I've given a lot to my job. I sometimes regret the amount of time that I've had to put in professionally and that's taken me away from my family. And I sometimes look back and think, "Gee I probably could have changed the balance – the work and family balance, in terms of hours".' He says his family are very supportive, but they have had a lot to bear. 'I guess if there was one area that ... I need to rethink it might be that one. Spend as much time with your family as you can', he says, 'because the strength of community is strong family'.

Andrew Scipione's optimism spreads well beyond his beloved Police Force, the communities he serves, or even the hopes he has for Generation Y. His quiet self-assurance stems from an unfaltering belief that life is not limited to the here and now, but has a trajectory towards eternity. 'The bigger God is in your life, the bigger your life is going to be', he says. 'And I've got this notion that God wants [us] to live big lives for him – give it [your] all; spend it all. Die empty because there's a refill coming when you go into eternity. God's got that covered; you don't need to keep anything in reserve. I'm just an ordinary kid from an ordinary part of Sydney with an ordinary life and yet God's done extraordinary things in my life.'

Le

'God was there,
even in the wilderness.'

h Hatcher

Television News Journalist

The incessant beeping of an alarm clock at 4am is enough to make even the most enthusiastic of early-risers wince. Yet this is the sound that greets Leigh Hatcher each day and it catapults him into a world of auto cues, breaking news, adrenalin bursts and live feeds. It is a place of makeup, bright lights, technology, and short grabs. All the world might be a stage, but this is an especially intense one. And people *are* watching.

He has tasted success and the trappings of television notoriety, but he also knows intimately the loneliness and crushing despair of a fall into near oblivion.

As the morning newsreader for pay TV station Sky News Australia, Hatcher presents rolling news bulletins across Australia and New Zealand. In over 30 years as a news journalist, Hatcher regards this current job as one of his favourites. And he has had some good ones. I well remember Hatcher reporting in each night in the mid-80s from various locations across Europe – Berlin, Dublin, Moscow, and London. I have an image of him in a long winter coat, signing off, 'This is Leigh Hatcher in Prague, (or Vienna or Budapest) for Seven News'. Hatcher fondly recalls those years as Channel Seven's Bureau Chief in London. It was the time of the Cold War and divided Europe, the IRA was 'very busy' and for Hatcher there were trips through Eastern and Western Europe every week. 'It was an eventful, intoxicating, demanding, exhausting, exhilarating life', he says.

Hatcher has experienced much success in his field and his CV would be the envy of any budding news journalist. On the day I meet him at a café in his local area he is not long off work, but looking relaxed, in the remnants of newsreader's attire – an open neck shirt and suit pants. He's ready to kick back into the weekend. He has the air of satisfied calm that success can breed in those who achieve it. He gives the impression of a man comfortable in his own skin.

Yet to hear Leigh Hatcher's story is to know that he takes nothing for granted, and that each day is a gift. He has tasted success and the trappings of television notoriety, but he also knows intimately the loneliness and crushing despair of a fall into near oblivion. Hatcher's demise came by way of Chronic Fatigue Syndrome (CFS) that hit him out of the blue and at the peak of his powers in the run-up to the Sydney Olympics, where he was to have had a key role at the Seven Network.

The illness left Hatcher virtually bedridden for two years. Unable to work, he lost his job, his income, his status, and his identity. Endless rounds of medical tests provided no answers. Meanwhile Hatcher endured wracking pain, and inexplicable, debilitating tiredness. The previously energetic, gung-ho reporter, TV presenter, father of four and regular swimmer, literally could no longer get off the couch. Utterly at a loss to explain what was going on, the early days of lethargy and inactivity stretched into weeks and months. He became so sick that a doctor friend of his later admitted he thought Hatcher was dying.

He had to the endure insensitivity and lack of understanding of friends and colleagues, a common experience of CFS sufferers and one that Hatcher found especially painful. Ill-informed advice, and scepticism that the illness was anything more than 'in his head', came from an ever-dwindling line of visitors. Mostly they offered unhelpful observations. Think of Job's friends and you might have an idea of what Hatcher had to endure from some.

'I'd spent 25 years reporting on people's lives being turned upside down', says Hatcher. 'And then it happened to me.' What he experienced was the deeply personal struggle with loss that nightly news presentations rarely penetrate.

One of the few things that never left Hatcher during his time of trial was the Christian faith he had held since he was a teenager. 'God was there even in the wilderness and almost the deeper you went into it, the more real he was – I had my view of God hugely enlarged', recalls Hatcher. Prior to the illness, Hatcher says he had 'God pretty much boxed up and sliced and diced, and everything neatly tucked away', and yet he found the experience of CFS wasn't neat or tidy and didn't fit what he now regards as a somewhat constrained framework of Christian belief. It was in this 'grey' of suffering that he most powerfully met God. 'Through my reading of the Bible, and other people's stories and reflections on God, over and over again, there were staggering ways in which God spoke to me. It wasn't in some spooky kind of way, but what I was reading in the pages of the Bible spoke so powerfully and so potently to the circumstances of each particular day', explains Hatcher. These moments Hatcher now describes as 'treasures in the darkness'.

Obviously, reading the Bible is something Hatcher takes seriously. Before he became unwell, he had taken a year's leave of absence to study theology and learn ancient Greek, the language of the New Testament. He went on to tutor students in Greek and also to learn Old Testament Hebrew. 'One of the things I love about the Bible [is that] it's no theoretical document written in a vacuum – it's life in all its glory and gory detail', he says.

Hatcher first came to faith in high school although he is quick to point out that his 'conversion' involved a long process – a journey that lasted years. He remembers the death of an uncle in his early teenage years as a defining moment. 'It was the first time that death had come anywhere near close to me and I found it an entirely shocking thing', he says. While not coming from a family of believers, Hatcher did attend the local Sunday school and youth group. It was only there, he says, that death was being dealt with in any way, shape or form and it was a catalyst to belief. 'For most of my life I've thought that was a pretty lame entry into the Christian faith, kind of being scared into it. However I've thought over the last few years I actually don't think it's so lame, for [death] is the issue that we all must deal with, and we all must have an answer to it. It strikes me, after both living out the Christian faith, and looking hard at other philosophies and outlooks, in the person of Jesus Christ we find the most authentic, historically viable and eternally hopeful answer to that.'

'God was there even in the wilderness and almost the deeper you went into it, the more real he was – I had my view of God hugely enlarged.'

Hatcher has been behind the microphone for some of the biggest stories of recent decades. As a very young and very green radio reporter, he stood on the steps of Australia's Parliament House at the announcement of the dismissal of the Whitlam Labor government in 1975. In that most enduring of Australian political images, it is possible to make out a bearded 20-year-old Hatcher in front of Whitlam, watching on as the representative of the Governor-General, David Smith, brought down the infamous declaration.

'With all the tough stuff and the sin in the world, also comes great beauty, and lavish provision, and a truly amazing creation and life.'

As a roving reporter for television news, Hatcher was on the scene soon after a deranged Wade Frankum opened fire in Strathfield shopping centre in Sydney's west in 1991, killing seven and wounding six. This was an event Hatcher found especially traumatic, given the closeness in age of some of the victims to his own daughters. 'It was a truly gruesome thing and ... it really rocked me', he says. Hatcher was in the newsreader's chair at Sky

News for the September 11 terrorist attacks in New York in 2001, and the Bali bombings of 2002. He was live to air in 2005 when the bodies of nine Australian service men and women, killed when their Sea King helicopter crashed on the Indonesian island of Nias, were returned home. They had been on a mercy mission to the earthquake-devastated area when they met their deaths. As the coffins were unloaded onto the tarmac, Hatcher struggled to maintain composure as he read the names of the dead from a single sheet of paper.

Through countless bulletins of mostly bad news, Hatcher says his faith has served to provide him with perspective. 'As far as the news goes, your job is often serving up lots of death, doom and destruction, so to have in the midst of that, a sense of a bigger picture and a higher purpose and a larger framework where God is in charge in all things', Hatcher says is a true comfort. 'With a Christian framework I understand myself, and my own sin, and I understand the sin of others. It's a story of hope stretching across an eternal time-line, not in the media snapshots that shape so much of our world view', he says.

When I ask him about the most appealing aspects of his Christian belief, Hatcher says it provides him with 'a sense of equilibrium and calm against the turmoil of the world – certainly the world that I inhabit and report on. It gives a coherent explanation of why the world is like it is and certain hope for the future. My outlook differs from an overemphasis on God's judgment that I think we could sometimes feel crushed with. ...Yes, there is God's judgment but there is also God's mercy. With all the tough stuff and the sin in the world, also comes great beauty, and lavish provision, and a truly amazing creation and life'.

The fast-paced world of news media is not one for the faint hearted, nor is it known for its sympathy to Christian belief. Hatcher has had to face many challenges in finding a healthy balance between his work and faith. He is clearly comfortable with the relationship, but acknowledges the pitfalls of ego and celebrity in the world of television. 'It's very easy to get swept away by that and imagine it's your identity, and reality. It's very good to have a family under those kinds of circumstances because they keep you very much grounded. I think that's a great danger, that you live out a totally unreal, and not so humble, kind of existence', suggests Hatcher.

The question of truth, especially in terms of the impression left by a story, has on occasion been an issue. Sometimes this has meant taking a stand and refusing a story. Once, on the way back from shooting a news item, Hatcher heard the radio promo for that story which he said had been completely beaten up and overturned. Hatcher got on the phone to the station to intervene and put a stop to the distortion. Hatcher's description of that moment being 'pretty tense' is surely an understatement. 'I doubt I would have gotten away with that as a 22-year-old', he admits.

The choices Hatcher has made relating to his family have been very significant. This has meant knocking back lucrative and enticing offers on more than one occasion, so as to allow more time for his family. Yes, he says, his Christian belief has been important in these decisions. 'My faith informs an outlook that says, "It's not about me"', he explains. 'If it was about me I'd have done lots of different things. But it's about them as well. As God relates to me in a merciful and generous manner, he has also put me in a position of being a father in my little outfit. I take that responsibility seriously – though I frequently fall short, I've go to say that. I remember sitting in one of my News Director's offices once and he was wistfully saying, "I've had a very successful career, I've earned a lot of money, I've got a great reputation, I want for nothing but I've got no relationship with my 21-year-old son".' That is why, says Hatcher, his own choices have been good ones.

Hatcher's recovery from his illness was gradual. There were many days when he wondered if he would ever regain his strength. But recover he did. 'About 90%', he thinks. The 'remnant' that he has been left with, he likens to the apostle Paul's famous 'thorn in the flesh'. Hatcher quotes 2 Corinthians 12 verse 9: 'My grace is sufficient for you for my power is made perfect in weakness'. It is this dependence on God that Hatcher believes is what he needed to learn, and what provides the key to a meaningful life. 'This is where I am fortunate being in my work – I see how ridiculous it is for people to imagine that they are in control. We love to be competent and confident, imagining we're in control of our lives and Christian people and church leaders are not immune from that. There's not a lot of humility in this age in which we live', he says. It is in finally learning to be dependent on God in daily life that Hatcher believes we create a healthy space in which to live. This is a space, he says where 'you've got a far more realistic view of both yourself and God. ... You get the relationship sorted out on an appropriate level so that you're dependent on God and humble before him'. What you find is that 'he is most merciful and loving'.

' ... I see how ridiculous it is for people to imagine that they are in control.'

It has taken years for Hatcher to come to terms with the disillusionment he felt in the way he was treated in his Christian community when he lost his health. For a long time this threatened to leave him bitter, but he now acknowledges that before getting sick, he too would have been suspicious, judging and lacking acceptance of someone in his situation. 'I would have been terrible to myself. I would have had to avoid myself very quickly', he laughs.

The lessons Hatcher learned from his wilderness experience were profound and life-changing. He describes his illness as 'life in the pit'. But he has a changed perspective because of what he went through. 'It has made me so much more of a compassionate person', he says. 'In my early days as a Christian, I thought God was so cranky and never happy with me and was always there when I'd trip up and fail. I thought God was much more interested in what I did – especially within the Christian community – than who I was.'

'And then I moved beyond that. I had this absolute transformation from being a useful, prominent person to being useless and in bed for much of each day. And I could give God nothing; I could achieve nothing for him – I was absolutely of no use to him. Yet I found him to be so much larger and so much lovelier; such an engaging God, meeting the needs and circumstances of each and every day.'

So what legacy would Leigh Hatcher most like to leave? 'The thing I would most hope for – really, the only thing I would hope for – would be for my kids to know the truth and reality of this faith, ... to see them embrace an authentic and enduring Christian faith that keeps feeding them through their university years and into their 30s, 40s and so on.' No doubt Hatcher hopes those closest to him are spared the type of painful lessons he has endured. But in another way, he embodies the notion of what can be gained from the hard road. 'I don't think you learn any quality lessons in life unless it's tough.'

Aar

'In the end it's not going
to matter how many
tournaments I won.'

Baddeley

Professional Golfer

The food and travel writer, AA Gill, on learning to play golf says, 'The moment you pick up a golf [club], you're faced with the realisation that this is an unnatural act. Of all the unnatural acts that might end in your ridicule, ostracism, penury, and humiliation, this is by far the most unnatural'.[4] Those of us, who have been lured into the golfing trap and played the game under the crushing illusion that we might actually get the hang of it one day, know exactly what he is talking about. Seduced by the immaculate cooch, the sweeping lawns of perfection, and the nirvana of a sub-par round (or even a vaguely respectable score card), we submit to the torture and cast ourselves upon the guillotine of golf's cruelty and shame. There is an air of inevitability about all this – lemmings waiting in line for a grizzly fate. That is why – and only those who have tried understand this – to watch one of the world's top golfers in action, truly is a thing of awe. Aaron Baddeley is one of those who have taken that most 'unnatural act' and turned it into something poetic.

In 1999, Baddeley shocked the sporting world, and perhaps even himself by winning the Australian Open Golf Championship at Royal Sydney. The first amateur to win the title in 39 years, he was 18 years old but looked even younger. Holding off seasoned champions Colin Montgomerie and Greg Norman to finish at 14-under, Baddeley not only displayed extraordinary dexterity in driving, putting and chipping, but astonishing nerve. In every sense he was a boy amongst men, but somehow he prevailed. As he accepted the trophy, Baddeley famously said, 'I would like to thank my Lord and Saviour Jesus Christ'. If the fact that a virtual schoolboy had wrestled the trophy from some of golf's biggest names sat a little uncomfortably, then the acceptance speech no doubt had the gathered throng shifting from leg to leg, and staring at the their feet not knowing where to look.

Fast-forward eight years. Ten days after I spoke with him in late 2007, he held aloft the Australian Masters trophy, after a tense four-hole play off with Daniel Chopra. Again Aaron spoke

---

4. A.A. Gill, *Previous Convictions*, (Phoenix paperbacks, 2006), page 30.

of his Christian faith. This time people were less surprised, more accepting. Even if his naked 'God talk' still makes people uneasy, Baddeley has earned his place at the table. When he speaks, people are more likely to listen. In the past five years he has struck up a friendship with the Australian Cricket Captain Ricky Ponting, who, it has to be said, is not known for drinking green tea and being in bed by nine. Evidently 'Punter' speaks regularly with Baddeley, happy to take advice from Baddeley on his golf swing. Such a relationship is testament to the respect in which Aaron is held within tight sporting circles.

... the acceptance speech no doubt had the gathered throng shifting from leg to leg, and staring at their feet not knowing where to look.

Recent years have produced significant changes in Aaron Baddeley's life. He looks and sounds older and wiser. He is married, more mature and settled. His swing is more consistent. And he has come through some difficult times when success eluded him to a point where he thought about quitting the game. What have not changed are his prodigious talent, his unfailing self-belief, and an overt commitment to his Christian faith.

After that precocious first win in 1999, Baddeley was invited to play in the U.S. Masters at Augusta and the U.S. Open. Despite missing the cut in both events, he returned to Australia later in the year to repeat the feat of 12 months prior, and go one better, winning both the Aussie Open and the prestigious Greg Norman Classic. These were heady days as Baddeley's name regularly appeared in sentences that included some of golf's greats. And then, he promptly vanished. This was not quite a 'call the missing person's unit' kind of disappearance, but Baddeley looked highly likely to slide into obscurity; becoming yet another subject of late night trivial pursuit questions in the collective smoky haze that is sporting memory. And he could hardly have been blamed for going down the same path as others for whom success came too early and in such abundance.

Baddeley looked highly likely to slide into obscurity; becoming yet another subject of late night trivial pursuit questions.

Choosing to take on the toughest circuit in the world, Baddeley went to America as an 18-year-old, and struggled to compete at that high level. 'The first few years of it were tough', says Aaron. 'I'd probably say they didn't live up to expectations. I guess because I was still young and I was growing in who I was and learning how to deal with that type of lifestyle. I would say those were the hardest times in my life, without a shadow of a doubt. At that time of my life, golf was everything – you know, it was my be-all and end-all', says Baddeley, admitting to an imbalance in his life that he has since overcome. 'I was away from home, I was homesick, I didn't have any friends because

I had just moved to a brand new country and it was rough. All my friends were at home here.'

Jack Newton, one of Australia's most successful golfers of the 70s and 80s and who knew Aaron in the junior ranks, was one of many who thought Aaron rushed into playing in America, when Europe might have provided a better grounding. 'He got his backside kicked a bit', says Jack of Aaron's first few years in the States. 'That quite often happens particularly to young golfers who suddenly get thrown into the big bad world in America where I think, to some extent, it's easy for young blokes to get tangled up in all the razzmatazz and stuff that goes on in the tour in America. Aaron has fought his way out of that hole though, and in the last couple of years he's played sensationally well', says Jack. 'Some people never come out the other side but he has, and is certainly a better player for it.'

The early years in the States were character-forming days, and Baddeley admits to being lonely and frustrated. 'There was a time there where I wanted to quit. And then I got back to my goals, and in my heart wanting to play good golf and wanting to win tournaments and I kept pressing on and as frustrating as it was, I kept practising and working at it. Just because I wasn't playing well, doesn't mean I wasn't in the exact position that God wanted me to be.' Long-time manager and friend Paul Galli, who wouldn't describe himself as a 'born again Christian' says of Aaron: 'He never lost sight of believing in himself and I have to say, I do believe his faith is a major factor in what kept him going'. Today, Baddeley is more than at home in the company of the world's best players. Tenth on the U.S. money earners list in 2007, he has established himself as a genuine contender for any major tournament. At time of writing he is ranked 18th in the world, and rising.

Raised in a church-going family, Baddeley regards his parents, Ron and Jo-Ann as enormously influential in him accepting Christianity for himself. 'The biggest thing was that they lived what they spoke', says Aaron. When a young Baddeley heard Australian Football legend Gary Ablett preach a sermon at a 'Youth Alive' meeting, he took the plunge. 'Even though I'd grown up in a Christian home, I felt like, "Tonight's the night I'm going to commit my life to Jesus"', he says. Reflecting on the way that initial commitment grew into something more substantial, Aaron says, 'Growing up, even though you would call me a Christian, I never really read my Bible and didn't really pray very much, so my relationship with God wasn't close, wasn't strong. In the past five, six, seven years I've ... grown in my knowledge and understanding of the Bible. And also grown in prayer. That's how it has changed. My relationship [with God] has gotten stronger and closer'. One gets the impression that Baddeley approaches his faith with the same single-mindedness that characterises his golf. He is an avid reader – largely of Christian books – and he quotes from Scripture frequently and accurately. He has been known to recite Bible verses to help clear his head of distractions while playing.

Sports journalist Peter FitzSimons frequently criticises Baddeley, or any other Christian athlete, for thanking God when they win. FitzSimons argues that to do so implies that the Creator cares more about one person's putting, backhand volley, jump shot, or cover drive than he does about world poverty and millions dying of AIDS. 'The real problem is when you draw attention to the notion that all glory belongs to God for helping you come first, the inherent assumption must be that he wasn't with the one who came second', writes FitzSimons. Feeling a degree of empathy with the complaint, I put it to Aaron for a right of reply. 'When I thank him it is like this, "Lord, thanks for what you do in my life, for allowing me to play this game for a living and I'm giving glory to you because without you in my life I wouldn't even be here"', explains Aaron. 'Whether I win, lose or miss the cut, I can walk away knowing that I have honoured God with my talent. It's not like God takes his attention and puts it solely on one individual. He's omnipresent, he can multi-task. He can do more than one thing at a time. So, while God could be giving a player extra peace during the time that he is playing well – like Zach Johnson who had great peace when he won the

U.S. Masters – God's also stirring on someone else's heart to go and help people over in Africa or something like that. He's doing both at the same time. He's not doing one thing and not the other.'

Baddeley says he feels called to play golf. He finds encouragement from Jesus' parable about the servant multiplying what he has been given rather than hiding it in a hole in the ground. 'I think the best thing that I can do is to use what [God] has given me', he says. 'If he has given me the talent to play golf, and he's called me to play golf, then I gotta play golf. That's what he's called me to do. And that's being obedient', he says. Without that call Aaron feels sure he would have given up when things were tough early in his career.

'Sports journalist Peter FitzSimons frequently criticises Baddelely, or any other Christian athlete, for thanking God when they win.'

And so it is with religious zeal that Baddeley approaches the task of being the very best player that he can be. Yet strangely, he manages to hold on to a perspective that belies this obsessive streak. Golf commentators and writers often speak of his steadiness and composure even when things have gone horribly wrong for him on the course. In 2007 he led Tiger Woods into the final round of the U.S. Open before a spectacular blowout saw him plummet out of contention. Even amidst such a shattering disappointment, writers spoke of Baddeley's level-headed optimism, and determination to learn from the experience. 'In the end it's not going to matter how many tournaments I won and stuff like that', says Aaron. 'I mean it is important to understand that. When I die I'm going to see Jesus and I want to know that I lived my life seeking his plans and what he wants me to be. Because my plans don't mean anything in the scheme of eternity.'

Even amidst such a shattering disappointment, writers spoke of Baddeley's level-headed optimism, and determination to learn from the experience.

Baddeley possesses a rare mix of immense self-confidence and talent combined with large doses of apparent humility, not the false humility that we are used to from robotic athletes who feel compelled to play down any achievement and to publicly attribute to luck any success they achieve. Baddeley knows he is an extremely gifted player. But at the same time he does a very convincing impersonation of a thoroughly polite, friendly, down-to-earth bloke. Those closest to Aaron speak of his sincerity, and his caring and well-rounded nature. He still catches up with long-time friends whenever he is home in Australia, placing high value on relationships that are not clouded by the dizziness of success and notoriety. '[Those friendships] are the best', Aaron explains. 'You know they were your friends before you were anything – not that playing golf makes you somebody – you just know that they are along because of who you are. They are along because they really care for you.'

Jack Newton, himself a great promoter of junior golf, is clearly impressed that Aaron thinks of more than just his own game. 'He is already putting something back into junior golf through his Aaron Baddeley International Junior Tournament', says Jack. 'He's got a genuineness about him that you've got to admire.'

Baddeley has a simple formula for keeping himself focused and on track, and it revolves around daily time spent reading the Bible and praying. This is what he says keeps his relationship with God strong, out of which flows growth as a person. 'Through that [relationship] comes a desire to serve, through that comes giving and generosity, through that comes humility, and through that comes character', explains Aaron. 'There are definitely times of struggle and times when your priorities get out of line a little bit', he admits. 'Yet if I can keep [God] as number one, then I'm OK. That's what's really important in everybody's life. He has to be number one – if that doesn't happen we are in trouble.'

Baddeley is quite an advocate for his faith, and works hard to present a positive image to the public. 'No matter what walk of life it is, whether as a Christian or an athlete or as a teacher or whatever, no-one likes a hypocrite', says Baddeley. 'A friend of mine says to me, "You can meet someone for three seconds and that memory will stick with them for a lifetime". That's important, you know; that's a big responsibility', Aaron says. Many of us would wince at the thought of our less glorious moments being scrutinised as representing the totality of even our own characters, let alone anything more substantial, but Aaron appears to wear the role lightly. Interestingly, when asked what he would most like to be remembered for, it is not golf that he speaks of. 'The number one thing would be that I was someone who had a close relationship with the Lord, who sought his plan and lived his life according to the Bible and was a sincere person.'

Paul Galli sees Aaron as courageous in being so public about his faith. 'I guess that makes some people uncomfortable in [Australia]', says Paul. 'In some ways it's more acceptable in America. He's well aware of what the feeling is, and what some people might say, but it's never bothered him.'

In an age of sports stars dominating headlines for drug-fuelled scandals, indulgent and reckless behaviour, Aaron cuts a refreshing figure. About the most offensive thing he has done is to commit some (admittedly serious) fashion crimes.

Sincerity is something Aaron values highly. Allan Meyer, himself a single figure handicap golfer who was Aaron's pastor in Mt Evelyn in Victoria and remains something of a mentor to Aaron, says 'There's not a fake bone in his body. He's exactly what he appears to be – transparent, genuine and very sincere'. In an age of sports stars dominating headlines for drug-fuelled scandals, indulgent and reckless behaviour, Aaron cuts a refreshing figure. About the most offensive thing he has done is to commit some (admittedly serious) fashion crimes, earning him the nickname 'Dresses', as in 'Dresses Baddeley'! He even seems to have toned that down in recent years, mercifully consigning lime green and pink trousers to the bottom of the locker.

Baddeley wouldn't be human if his current jet-setting lifestyle didn't present some temptations. The biggest of these, he says, are things like 'getting wrapped up in what people think of you, and in what the media says about you and how much money you make, wearing the right clothes, driving the newest and latest car; things like that. It is so easy to get wrapped up in that. I guess that would be something you always need to keep a check on. That's where Richelle is so great. She just doesn't care. She is fantastic', explains Aaron, referring to the influence of his wife of three years.

Unlike other sports, golf is a game in which players can realistically plan for long careers. So what would life be like without golf for Aaron? 'I think that it would definitely be a lot different if I couldn't play golf, because my whole life that's what I have done', he explains. 'Put it this way, I'm going to play golf until God tells me to do otherwise. And I believe if there is a time like that, he will take away my passion for the game. That love of the game won't be there. If it's going and doing missions in Africa or something, then God will really give me a passion and a heart for that. So I think I really wouldn't miss golf in that case because God would have given me a passion for something else.'

In the meantime, Aaron continues to be determinedly who he is – thankful, thoughtful, and completely *un*natural in wielding the golf club.

J

'I've always had a very real sense that it's not my superior who decides what will happen to me, but ultimately it is God.'

igadier (ret)
n Wallace

Former Head of SAS
and Special Forces

I should have been better prepared. Had I been trained in the world of 'situational awareness', I would have been thinking ahead. I would have known what was coming and been able to instantly assess all the data, and react to my circumstances appropriately. As it was, I placed myself in a compromising position and panicked at the crucial moment. I'd arranged to meet Jim Wallace at 5pm at a café on the northern fringe of Sydney Harbour. I love my coffee, but have learnt through hard experience that any caffeine after about lunchtime will leave me staring wide-eyed at the ceiling at 3am. As Jim sauntered to the counter to place his order – an emphatic long black – the seriousness of the situation rushed in upon me. I couldn't possibly order a decaf, soy latte in front of the former head of the SAS and Special Forces in the Australian Army and hope to carry any dignity into our impending conversation. 'Make that two', I said. A long night lay ahead.

From the time he entered Duntroon Military College as a fresh faced teenager, to his eventual retirement from the army in 2001, Jim Wallace was a pin-up success story for the armed forces. During a distinguished 32-year career as a first-rate officer, topping his peer group and being promoted through the ranks at the first opportunity, Wallace rose to become commander of the army's mechanised brigade of tanks, armoured vehicles and 3000 men. He also commanded the elite SAS and Special Forces for the army – his defining role, and what he is most known for. He served in the Middle East with the United Nations as an unarmed observer, and graduated from the British Army Staff College and the Australian College of Defence and Strategic Studies. In 1984, he was made a Member of the Order of Australia for his services to counter-terrorism, after commanding the terrorist squadron, including preparing and holding the counter terrorist response capability during the Brisbane Commonwealth Games. While commanding the SAS Regiment some four years later he would be the driving force in establishing regional counter terrorist forces, an initiative that drew scepticism at the time, but one that has been well and truly vindicated by 9/11 and Bali. Had he not resigned, Wallace could have reasonably expected to be competing for chief of the army at some point.

For much of his life, Jim Wallace has been spoiling for or engaging in a fight – firstly in the army and now as head of the Australian Christian Lobby. Yet no combative nature is on display when I meet him. He is warm, engaging, self-effacing and understated. Nonetheless, he exhibits qualities you would rightly expect from someone of his standing – confidence, self-assurance and strength. A father of two, Wallace is a rugby fanatic, playing his last game when he was 45. He still looks fit and energetic. With the manners of an officer – he is overly helpful with the surprised waitress – but without airs or pretensions, Wallace reflects a demeanour typical of the Australian Army that has made it so popular around the world.

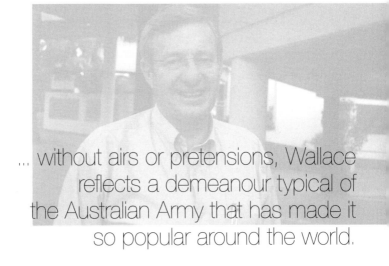

... without airs or pretensions, Wallace reflects a demeanour typical of the Australian Army that has made it so popular around the world.

Unlike many who make it as an officer, Wallace emerged from humble beginnings. The son of a World War II soldier who served at Tobruk and Milne Bay, Wallace was born in Sydney but moved to the Tweed Valley in northern New South Wales when he was very young. After two retail businesses literally disappeared under the flooding Tweed River, the family faced the ignominy of having to live in a migrant hostel for a couple of years. There were no old school tie connections to be forged, but rather the hard-edged and earthy surrounds of Balmoral State High School in Brisbane, in which Wallace rose to prominence, holding every leadership position available including School Captain in his final year. 'I think we had the highest pregnancy rate in the state, but it all went past me, I missed it all', laughs Jim.

'Stupidly we went in with them and when we got there, 1500 people just closed in around us, an angry mob.'

Wallace left school in 1969 and headed straight for The Royal Military College Duntroon where the training and education of all Australian Army officers begins. It was in his early days there, when home on leave that he first encountered friends who were Christian. As a boy, Wallace remembers taking himself off to church a few times, but really had no other grounding in religion. After initially regarding Christianity as an unnecessary crutch, a friend's challenge to consider the implications of the faith actually being true, proved profound. 'In the end I simply got down on my knees and asked Christ into my life', he says. 'And from then on, I have found he certainly is a crutch when you need him, and everyone needs a crutch. But also, as the builder of the car, he knows how many gears it's got and what it can do in each gear and he pushes it out to its limit, but not, if we stay with him, beyond its limit. And that's what I've found in the things that I've done, particularly in the SAS and Special Forces, and indeed setting up the Australian Christian Lobby from scratch. That was a terrific thing to know and be able to put your faith in.'

What can't be missed in Jim Wallace's story is his deep sense of trust in God. This has been born out of experience and compelling life circumstances. Wallace earned a reputation in the army as an innovative and bold operator. He credits much of this to his strong sense of self; emanating from the security his faith provided him. 'In the army or any hierarchical system you can become very dependent on patronage and what your boss thinks of you', says Wallace. 'But I've always had a very real sense that it's not my superior who decides what will happen to me, but ultimately it is God. [This means] you can afford to take risks; you can afford to be an imaginative and creative type of leader because you are not worried so much about the fear of failure, which I think a lot of people are.'

Undoubtedly the biggest test of Wallace's faith came when working for the UN in the Middle East. While he was acting as a UN observer, the PLO in Lebanon kidnapped him. One of his jobs was to report on violations of the ceasefire where the Palestinian refugee camps had been bombed or shelled usually by Christian militia forces or Israelis.

When working with the Red Crescent in October 1980, two shells landed in a nearby refugee camp. At the urging of the Red Crescent workers, and against his better judgement, Wallace and a colleague immediately headed into the camp. Protocol would normally be to allow 36 hours after such an incident for the heat to subside. 'Stupidly we went in with them and when we got there, 1500 people just closed in around us, an angry mob. There had been an old man killed with a shell and another shell had hit a car in which a mother and daughter were travelling and had killed them both.'

'And they jostled us up to a meeting hall in the middle of the refugee camp and as we went up the steps, a young boy of about 14 came and grabbed the sleeve of my shirt and dragged me down the steps to the car in which the mother and daughter had just been killed. The bodies had been taken out but the blood was still there because it was only about 20 minutes later. And he grabbed my hand and he rammed it into the blood. And it was like he was saying, "This is your fault mate, you are not stopping this, you are stopping us getting in there but you are not stopping this happening to us".'

Wallace and his colleague were then taken into the meeting hall where about 30 men from the village guarded them while an executive group in a side room was deciding whether to execute them or not. Wallace says that as a young SAS captain you really think you can beat the world. 'But in this case I really couldn't do anything. All I could do was just remember how big our God is, you know. I brought back to mind those verses in Isaiah 40 verse 12, I think it is, where we are told that God holds the waters of the world in the palm of his hand. He measures the mountains in scales and the hills in a balance. He marks off the heavens with the span of his hand. This is a big God. And I just put my future and my safety in the hands of that big God and after some hours, I can't remember how long it was now, probably about 12 hours, might have been a bit less, they just let us go.' This was a very close call. Only a few months before, two Irishmen had been killed in similar circumstances, and when Wallace returned to Australia, an American observer was tortured and hanged. 'It was a really good lesson in terms of faith', says Wallace. 'I just felt a sense of peace that it was going to work out – I couldn't see how. I mean if I were them I wouldn't have let us go.'

Wallace seems always to have had an unshakeable belief in himself well suited to the positions he attained. On his first day in command of the SAS, he stood in front of the men, and declared that he would make his decisions from a Christian paradigm and while he wouldn't march them to chapel each week, they should be clear that's where he was coming from. One of his first moves was to ban strippers in the Officer's Rec. Club on ANZAC day. Shortly after this, he outlawed pornography in the regiment. 'I thought I'd almost get a rebellion in some quarters', says Wallace. But instead he received only thanks from many of the men, and especially, but not surprisingly, the wives. Wallace is conservative by nature, but is a strong believer that traditional Christian values are just good for relationships generally. 'They're decent values', he says, 'and they are deeply rooted in a lot of people'.

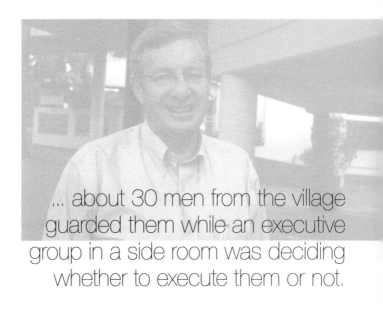

... about 30 men from the village guarded them while an executive group in a side room was deciding whether to execute them or not.

Major General Michael Jeffery, the Governor General of Australia from 2003-2008, was a Commanding Officer in the Special Air Service when Jim Wallace was in charge of the free falling parachuting troop. 'I see him as one of the most highly principled ... men that I have ever met, as well as being a natural leader', says Jeffrey of Wallace. Jeffrey says Wallace brought a sharp mind and professional approach to all tasks, along with deep loyalty to those above and below him. This, he says 'inspires automatic trust in everyone he meets'.

An obvious question for Wallace to address is that of matching up destructive military force with the Christian call to turn the other cheek and model the sort of love Christ displayed. Is there a tension in this dynamic? 'I sorted this out pretty early as you have to as a Christian in the military', he says. 'I suppose this was crystallised for me through a mate at Duntroon who became a Christian about the same time that I did. He was a very good soldier and after about three years of soldiering he decided he was a pacifist and he got out of the army. And he used to still come to our military Christian fellowship and he used to give me a hard time because I wasn't just in the army I was in the worst part of it', laughs Jim. 'So I said to him one night, "Well Bob if the enemy are coming down through northern Australia, you're not going to join the army again?" He said, "No". I said, "We're in the ACT; they're at the end of the street; they're going to have their way with your daughters, and kill your wife. Are you going to join the army now? Are you going to defend your family?" And to stay true to his pacifist conviction, he had to say "No". Now I don't know if it makes me a better or worse Christian, better or worse man, but I couldn't do that. And so I've no hesitation at all about the role of military force in this fallen world in which we live.'

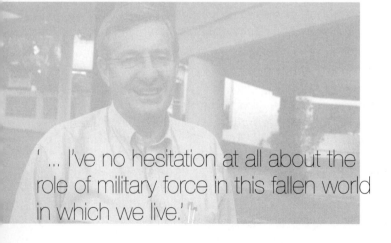

' ... I've no hesitation at all about the role of military force in this fallen world in which we live.'

Wallace gained immense respect from those with whom he served. This has perhaps emerged from an overt love for the institution and the people in it. Long-serving member of the SAS, Peter Lutley, who served under Wallace, says it is a tough road for a young officer to come in to lead elite SAS soldiers who are often experienced, cynical and extremely confident. '[They] have to prove themselves to earn respect', says Lutley – something he says Wallace did very successfully. 'The best officers make good decisions in stressful times, and Jim was one of those guys. ...There are very few like Jim. He was a sharp operator. [Someone like that] enables you to do your job, trusting that at the top the right decision will be made. He was firm but fair, and importantly could laugh at himself as well.'

Wallace says he has seen the best and worst of human nature during his time in the military. Overwhelmingly his experience with his own soldiers was positive. On his visits to Rwanda and Somalia where his men were serving, he found it heartening to see the compassion the soldiers offered – especially to children. 'They'd be down in Kibeho guarding people they were meant to be guarding, and then turning around and carrying a young child to a medical facility somewhere. Incredible compassion', says Wallace.

The army was a life to Wallace, and yet his Christian convictions took priority. At the height of his career – and with promotion to Major General imminent – Wallace felt called into another field altogether. 'I'd been sitting there thinking, "Why isn't the church influencing society more, and government more, and legislation more … and God convicted me of the fact that it's no good sitting there complaining about it, you've got to go out and do something about it.' In 2001 Wallace left the army to set up the Australian Christian Lobby (ACL) – an organisation that seeks to influence government, business and the community generally, to better acknowledge Christian values. The birth of the organisation sprung from Wallace's sense of a disproportionate amount of influence held by minority groups. The aim is to activate the Christian constituency to the point where government sees it as something to be taken seriously, and whose opinion and voice needs to be heeded. These days Wallace frequently appears on news and current affairs programmes for both TV and radio, speaking on behalf of the cause.

To the charge that organisations like the ACL are legislating morality, Wallace has an emphatic response. 'This is a secular democratic country, and we don't want ... to be trying to put the church over the public square. [But] somebody's morality gets legislated. There's no moral-free legislation ... and if the church isn't in there ensuring Christian morality is at least influencing legislation, then other people's will be.'

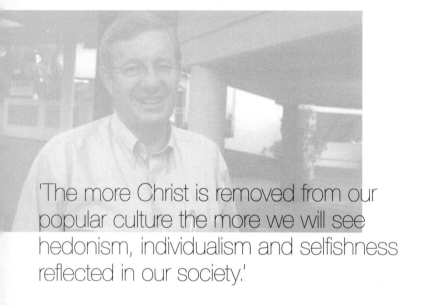

'The more Christ is removed from our popular culture the more we will see hedonism, individualism and selfishness reflected in our society.'

In Wallace's mind this is not merely moral crusading, but an attempt to correct an imbalance in our culture. Distancing himself from the American Christian Right's myopic focus on moral questions, Wallace sees theological reasons for a broader agenda. 'Governments are asked to govern with both justice and righteousness', he says. 'Christian influence should pervade and reach into both sides of politics. I don't think it's a case of the right or the left having a proprietary call on God. And we as Christians have to reflect that. ... On the whole, the Christian church should stay nonpartisan.'

A sense of what traditional values can contribute to the nation and the damage left by their loss is a powerful motivator for Wallace. 'The more Christ is removed from our popular culture the more we will see hedonism, individualism and selfishness reflected in our society', he says. 'It hasn't yet reached epic proportions but I think we are all seeing it, particularly in the breakdown of relationships. When a culture says, "It's all about me" and allows relationships to be reduced to that, then children especially become the casualties and we see that all the time.'

There is much that Jim Wallace gave up to take on his current role. For someone in such a senior position with a large staff, huge responsibility and corresponding trappings of military notoriety, it can't have been easy to start from scratch in a small office and relative anonymity. Perhaps the cruellest come-down of all was the arduous journey from Business Class to Economy when flying! You couldn't blame him for the occasional glance back to his former life. 'I must admit as I have seen the army in a high rate of operational activity and realised that I could have been in the middle of all that, it has been hard', says Wallace. Yet the conviction he gained as a young man at Duntroon has never left him. 'I've got no doubts that this is what God wanted me to do. I think God honours our decisions made honestly for him.'

Bru

'My experience of God... was overwhelmingly one of being held up; of being prevented from sinking.'

Robinson

Physician, author
Professor of Medicine

Meet Bruce Robinson. At 57 he has over 30 years' experience as a chest physician and is an internationally renowned Professor of Medicine. He is a world leader of research into asbestos-induced cancer; developing the first blood test for early detection of mesothelioma – a particularly nasty version. Among his many accolades for study in this field is the Wagner Medal awarded in 2004 for the 'individual who has made the greatest contribution to mesothelioma research internationally'. He leads a team of scientists who have produced eight world firsts in tumour therapies and is in demand as a speaker at medical conferences around the world. He has twice been awarded 'Teacher of the Year' at the University of Western Australia's School of Medicine. He has written over 160 scientific papers, and 25 chapters for books in his field. Following the Boxing Day tsunami in 2004, Robinson embarked on several trips to Aceh in Indonesia providing medical care, training in respiratory medicine and disaster preparedness. He co-founded the International Skills and Training Institute for Health, providing training in medicine and nursing to post-tsunami regions of Indonesia.

Robinson's interests spread well beyond medicine. An accomplished Australian Rules footballer in his youth, he went on to become a premiership-winning coach in the Western Australian Amateur Football League establishing a record 52-game winning streak. He is the author of a best-selling book *Fathering in the Fast Lane* and these days is called upon to give addresses around the world on the subject. He is proficient in four languages. I could go on. One has to wonder if he ever manages to sleep.

Armed with these facts, I prepare to meet the man. It's early summer when we sit down to talk in his home in the Perth suburb of Shenton Park. The professor is bare foot, wearing an Indonesian beer T-shirt, and what appears suspiciously like Stubby shorts. He looks and sounds like the old footballer that he is. Nothing in his appearance or manner betrays the esteem in which he is held in his community. He is extremely down-to-earth. His home sits comfortably in a picturesque and wealthy suburb, but is by no means elaborate. Robinson's children are all grown up now but they're still at home. There is warmth to the place, and ample signs of the hurly-burly of family life. At various points in the conversation we are joined by his adult son who breezes in and out, and his wife who leaves to counsel a distressed neighbour. He's not sure if his daughter is upstairs or not.

Despite his many and varied achievements, it is noticeable that he is most animated when talking about fathering, life-long friendships and his family. He is self-aware and conscious of his faults, especially those he possessed as a younger man.

'The professor is bare foot, wearing an Indonesian beer T-shirt, and what appears suspiciously like Stubby shorts.'

There is something very appealing about someone so accomplished and yet so unaffected. The positive side of Australian cynicism and egalitarianism provides a sense of being grounded that's worth holding on to. It's not surprising that Robinson possesses this quality given his background.

He grew up on the baking sandy Swan coastal plain in working class Bassendean – a suburb of Perth that in the 1950s sat on the fringe of the metropolitan area. Robinson remembers the bush beyond the playground of his school. 'Smoke rose from Aboriginal campfires and there was nothing between that and Darwin', he says.

As a kid he ran 'feral' around the neighbourhood with his friends while their fathers worked in local factories. He remains friends with a number of the boys from this time. Robinson remembers this as a blissful existence of freedom, community, stability and love.

'Even when I was a kid I would climb up on my parent's roof in the evening and look at the stars and try to contemplate the infinity of the universe ... and try to grasp it, purely from a scientific point of view, not searching for God or anything. So I've always been a questioner.'

Talking to Robinson about his childhood, I'm reminded of Conn and Hal Iggulden's *Dangerous book for Boys* – now globally popular for promoting an alternative to a computer-game generated, virtual-reality childhood. It's about getting outside in the mud, relishing in nature, playing sport and building billycarts and swing ropes. It's about all things healthy, energising and at times dangerous. 'We swam in the dirty brown water of the river flowing out of the hills, and we ran through the bush, and rode our bikes through the bush tracks', recalls Robinson. 'We found little streams and dammed them up, and made dirt tracks here and there for competitions on our bikes. We played a lot of sport. … You'd disappear in the morning and all they'd say would be, "Be back by five for dinner". You could have drowned and no-one would have known.'

Robinson says his dad was his hero growing up and despite the fact that he often drank too much, was 'a good dad, ahead of his time in many ways'. Growing up in a stable and loving home is something people typically come to appreciate later in life, and Robinson looks back on a rich childhood, despite relative poverty. 'We were dirt poor so we couldn't afford a TV or a car and ate cheap food like rabbit', recalls Robinson. 'A fundamentally happy childhood gives you that feeling that you're actually worth being around; your ego's nurtured [but] all that happens without you knowing it.'

Robinson speaks glowingly of his working class roots, and says he is completely at home in that environment. Yet he couldn't have followed his father into factory life. He had big dreams. 'I've always been a thinker about why things are the way they are', explains Robinson. 'Even when I was a kid I would climb up on my parent's roof in the evening and look at the stars and try to contemplate the infinity of the universe … and try to grasp it, purely from a scientific point of view, not searching for God or anything. So I've always been a questioner.' It is no surprise that Robinson didn't merely practise medicine, but threw himself into research, eventually gaining a Doctorate in Medicine in Washington DC. 'The practise of medicine is to ask the one question, "What is this, what is the diagnosis?" and then you give the right treatment. … But I have a second question and that is, "Why is this so?". That's research. And I've always been that way. "Why is the universe here?" "Why is the body so complex?"', explains Robinson.

It was the latter question that challenged his understanding of the largest questions of life and existence as a young medical student. Having not come from a church-going family, Robinson got something of a grounding in Christian teaching as a young boy attending Sunday school. 'Enough to give me a platform for consideration', he says. The complexity of the body gave Robinson reason to accept the argument that there must be a designer. He concluded that there was just too much detail and intricacy for this to be an accident. 'It seems a leap of faith to believe it was all chance', he explains, fully aware of the irony. 'So that's when I became a committed Christian at the age of 19', recalls Bruce. 'The choice was clearly there – you're either in or out of this thing. There's no tokenism and I made that decision with some fear and trembling. I thought I'd lose all my friends. I was in the in-crowd.' Robinson became what he describes as a 'full-on' Christian at that time. 'I was evangelising, and singing in groups, down at the beach. And I knew it all too, of course!'

Over time, Robinson grew increasingly uncomfortable with who he'd become. He believes the problem was a lack of authenticity. 'I had got into a leadership position too early and as a consequence I kept doing things because I thought I should. I kept being the sort of person I was supposed to be. I kept saying the things I was supposed to say, regurgitating dogma that I was being fed. And I thought, "Where's the real me in all this?".'

At the age of 25, having been a Christian for six years, Robinson largely abandoned his faith, and left on a backpacking tour of Europe, Asia and North America. He describes himself as being like a sugar cube dissolved in a cup of coffee – his Christian culture. Travelling enabled him to extract himself from that culture and 're-crystallise the sugar cube': to reflect on who he really was and what he wanted to be.

The movement towards this self-understanding was by no means instant, and involved a three-year journey across the globe. A chance meeting with a New Zealand couple in Thailand proved to be a seminal moment for Robinson. During that period he was examining and wrestling with the 'God is dead'

literature that claimed Christianity was all a myth. The pair
told him about a Christian study centre in Switzerland, called
L'Abri and drew him a 'mud map' on a scrap of paper of how to
get there. L'Abri was the headquarters of American philosopher
and writer, Francis Schaeffer, who TIME magazine called one
of the most significant Christian thinkers of the 20th century.
Two years later, using that same scrappy map, Robinson found
his way there.

What emerged from that time was a
newfound faith stripped of any pretence,
but stronger. 'I try to avoid the BS now',
declares Robinson.

Studying under Schaeffer was a turning point for Robinson.
'He'd say, "We give honest answers to honest questions", and
to be in an environment like that was wonderful. So I found
again the strong foundations philosophically for Christianity.'
What emerged from that time was a new-found faith stripped
of any pretence, but stronger. 'I try to avoid the BS now',
declares Robinson.

Two key sticking points for many people in terms of accepting
Christian faith are the questions of science: 'Hasn't science

removed belief in the supernatural?' and suffering: 'How could a God who is good and kind and all-powerful allow the suffering we witness and experience?' Bruce Robinson has been immersed in both of these issues for most of his adult life, and yet his belief remains firm. He has a team of 25 people working in high-tech biological science cloning genes. A third of his time is spent as a physician frequently treating lung cancer patients. 'I'm dealing with people who are suffering all the time', he explains. 'They're dying and they often die in a lot of pain. ... When it's a dad who's dying, and I can hear his kids outside in the waiting room or I know his wife, and they're weeping in front of me; I suffer from that too.'

'... I never try to give people a theological explanation of suffering. I hold their hand and weep with them and I say, "It's hard".'

Robinson remembers working in Indonesia after the Boxing Day tsunami as one of his most intense confrontations with human struggle and loss. 'The amount of suffering was mind-boggling', he says. 'Some days, I just had to shut the door and weep. Yet despite all this exposure to high-quality science, and intense suffering, I'm still a Christian. I think suffering is a difficult issue and I never try to give people a theological explanation of suffering. I hold their hand and weep with them and I say,

"It's hard". That's all I mostly do. You know that's a bit of a wimpy sort of response but no, I just weep with those who weep; I don't want to sound too theological ... but I just find suffering is a difficult thing to deal with theologically and personally.'

Robinson has had his own encounters with pain. He managed to almost sever both legs and nearly bled to death in a backyard DIY disaster involving a circular saw. He endured months of multiple operations, skin grafts and a neuralgic pain that he says was worse than the original injury. But it was during this time that his faith took on even greater meaning and clarity.

'As much as I intellectualise Christianity as a scientist', says Robinson, 'my experience of God personally, un-quantifiably, subjectively at that time was overwhelmingly one of being held up; of being prevented from sinking when I was suffering. It was such a powerful experience of God's presence. I can tell you that it was a subjective sense of the love of God looking out for me during a time of suffering. I mean how do you measure that? You can't. How can you convey that? Someone will explain it away with some [scientific, biological] explanation.'

'But I've had lesser experiences of God's love since then. ... So why am I still a Christian? It's an intellectual thing, partly. I still find that the arguments are pretty solid for Christianity being true. They're not incontrovertible. They're not completely rock solid such that you'd be called stupid if you didn't agree with them, but they're pretty profound and pretty strong. But the second thing is my experience of God in my journey of life, which is subjective and therefore unmeasurable, but is quite profound. These days if I'm in church singing a song about the love of God, I will weep. Because I feel it, you know, I can feel it as I sing. I can't finish the song – soppy old bastard I am!'

Robinson has led a life of broad interests and passions, and at each point his Christian faith has been either the catalyst or the flavour of his activity. Coaching Australian Rules football was not only a deep passion and enjoyment, but also a place in which he could live his faith. 'I coached footy because I love footy', he says. 'I loved coaching and I loved the guys I coached and I'm very close to them all still. I tried to be an authentic Christian in it all and by that I mostly mean treating them all as human beings and not as slaves to my coaching ambitions.'

On a camping holiday in 2004, the news of the tsunami came through. When the death toll climbed to 60 000, Robinson picked up his mobile phone and volunteered to go. 'In this team in Aceh, there were 120 Indonesians and one Aussie, which is why I learned to speak Indonesian so fast', he laughs. 'First of all it was an act of compassion, a desire to help but I also knew that Aceh is home to largely fundamentalist Muslim ... [ideology] within the most populous Sunni Muslim country in the world. And I know they get a distorted view of Christianity and I thought, "Well, if I can go up there and show love, at least I will show that this is what Christianity is about". I'm not trying to proselytise, I'm just trying to show some kindness.'

Robinson maintains enthusiasm for life and a determination not to always do the expected or the conventional. 'I've had to zig a couple of times when the world was telling me to zag', he says. 'The advice I would give to a young person is "follow your heart". ...[If] something looks comfortable and easy and the right opportunity, [but] your heart says it's not the right thing, don't do it. If students or young doctors tell me they want to take a year off medical school and go backpacking, or be a musician for a few years or open a vineyard or something, I say do it! I do, however, give another piece of advice which is about being intentional in life about the things that matter.' The things that matter, according to Robinson, are all to do with relationships – family, friends and ultimately God.

Robinson acknowledges that Christians don't always lead rich family lives compared to the rest of the population, but suggests that they ought to be able to. The reason, he says: self-understanding, confession and repentance are all required in healthy relationships. 'Each of those steps is fundamental to Christianity', he says.

These ideas have heavily influenced his advocacy of the critical importance of good fathering. This side-project has produced not only a book, but a DVD that is distributed to all schools in Western Australia and has found a receptive audience across the country and overseas. He has delivered talks to over 100 groups on this topic that is clearly a passion for him.

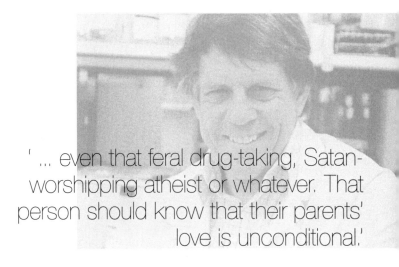

' ... even that feral drug-taking, Satan-worshipping atheist or whatever. That person should know that their parents' love is unconditional.'

One of Robinson's favourite passages in the Bible is the story of the prodigal son from Luke's Gospel, which he says is a summary of what a good father should be. 'I think there are three fundamental things that a father should be for his children. The first is, he should always be there for them. Street kids feel like there's no-one there for them and kids who commit suicide sometimes say, "There's no-one on my side". A dad needs to tell his kids, and show them, he's always going to be there for them. You can't stop them from making mistakes. You can always be there for them. The second thing is that your love for them doesn't depend on how well they do at school, or at sport or even their personality or their looks. And the third thing is that they are really special, even that feral drug-taking, Satan-worshipping atheist or whatever. That person should know that their parents' love is unconditional; that their parents really appreciate their specialness. And those happen to be three characteristics that God has, and they are the three overwhelming characteristics that God wants of us as fathers.'

'The father of the prodigal son didn't go and rescue the kid, but that kid knew that his dad would be there for him when he came home and indeed his dad was there. He saw his son afar off, he was watching the horizon. That's unconditional love; we call that grace, and that's what the prodigal son's father showed his son. Then he threw a party and he put a ring on his finger and a robe and made him feel special. So he cut away all that discipline and judgementalism. You're left with a wonderful rich image of what a father should be to his children – and a mother for that matter.'

'We've got God's model for that. He knows every bit of DNA in your body, you don't have to be more special than anyone else, you're just special. You are utterly unique, a unique creation. And I love that.'